3/95

The Habit of Rivers

Ted Leeson

Lyons & Burford, Publishers

The Habit of Rivers

Reflections on Trout Streams and Fly Fishing

Printed in the United States of America

Design by Kathy Kikkert

10 9 8 7 6 5 4 3 2

Leeson, Ted.
The habit of rivers: reflections on trout streams
and fly fishing / Ted Leeson.
p.   cm.
ISBN 1-55821-300-7
1. Trout fishing—Oregon.   2. Fly fishing—Oregon.
3. Rivers—Oregon.   I. Title.
SH688.U6L44   1994
799.1'755—dc20   93-42054
                                              CIP

To my Mother
For my Father and Mark

It is for such things that we were placed on this careening mudball.

—*Thomas McGuane,* An Outside Chance

Contents

Acknowledgments

At some level, all books are essentially collaborations. Much as a writer may call the work his own, other people have inevitably, and fortunately, been involved. I am grateful for the opportunity to acknowledge their contributions; one lives to incur such debts.

First, thanks to Nick Lyons, who, for reasons that will forever remain mysterious, had confidence in this project before a word of it was ever on paper, and during its completion, performed the various offices of editor, advisor, critic, midwife, and friend.

Thanks as well to Dave Hughes, who first encouraged, then urged me to write this book.

I am grateful to the friends, family, and fishing companions who have, in many ways, helped bring this book about. My thanks to Jean Archer, J. T. and Polly Campbell, Chris Camuto, Rich Daniels, Adelheid Fischer, Clark Harrison, George Hopper, Darrel Martin, Brian McGinley, Lisa Norris, Bill Potts, Bill and Andrea Rowland, Jim Schollmeyer, and particularly to Larry Stauffer, for his insatiable desire to explore.

And a special thanks to Lizard, who goes way back to the beginning.

Some debts are so vast and pervasive that they can scarcely be assessed, let alone repaid. Next to them, the word "thanks" seems absurdly small. I am deeply grateful to my wife, Betty Campbell, and my brother, Greg Leeson—foremost among fishing companions, my wisest teachers, and most beloved of friends, without whom, there is nothing.

Lastly, to Ted, Danny, and Meg, the small school of nephews and nieces who dart everywhere around the edges of this book, happily oblivious to it all, but a constant reminder that the past is not always gone and the future not always a secret.

Introduction

Every life has its points of fixity, certain small stillnesses in the incessancy of the world that anchor us with a sense of continuity and location. They are points of vantage and reference, places to stand from which the patterns of the past might be read and those of the future, perhaps, dimly inferred. For whatever reason, by karma or coincidence, such points in my own life have always centered upon rivers and streams and, above all, upon fly fishing for trout. Trout streams tug at the mind with an insistent, contradictory pull, presenting both a plain and perfect simplicity and a subtle link to sources of hidden significance; fundamentally alike, yet endlessly variable, they offer the solace of the familiar and the inexhaustible fascination of a thing that can never fully be known. There was a time that I didn't fish, but I cannot remember it.

Ten years ago, I moved west from Virginia to Oregon, recently married, with a new job and the probationary sense of promise that often accompanies change. Fishing wasn't the main reason for coming, but to get my bearings amid these new circumstances, I turned first to what I knew best. With a second-hand camper, a third-hand pickup, and an old wooden driftboat, I looked to rivers and fish as a way of gaining some initial access to an unfamiliar landscape that had suddenly become home. I found trout, steelhead, and salmon, and in time understood them well enough to manage a foothold in the fishing and so in the place itself. But the most consequential discovery was, in a way, the smallest—the simple fact that the fishing here never stopped. Each time it appeared as though the season had played itself out and I thought about shelving the tackle, some unexpected opportunity arose, an elsewhere or otherwise that postponed what I assumed to be inevitable. Month after month, I'd learn of another river, another run of fish, another season just reaching its peak. In a place as biologically and geographically varied as this one, somewhere, passable weather and good fishing always managed to coincide. If you employed a little imagination and the right gear, the angling year never ended.

This was a wholly unanticipated stroke of fortune, and its most obvious and immediate result was that I spent an unseemly amount of time on rivers. Gradually, though, and indirectly, a second, less direct consequence began to emerge. Bit by bit, the prospect of uninterrupted fishing began to reshape my perception, not merely of the seasons, but of seasonality. Time unfolded differently. In some respects, I ventured to Oregon for a new beginning and found a place that held out an endless succession of new beginnings, one after another, as rivers, lakes, landscapes, and fish came continuously into season. The year unrolled with a perpetual forward momentum that you could ride like a wave.

This new and unaccustomed sense of seasonality is the circumstance that occasioned this book, though not, strictly speaking, its subject. Instead, these chapters are about the consequences and significances of the idea, about seasons as spaces and landscapes as times, about a certain vision of fishing and fishing as a certain habit of vision, about rivers that express interior geographies as much as exterior ones.

To some temperaments, fishing appeals most deeply as an approach to a web of relations that give shape and coherence to the natural world. Fly fishing in particular embraces the kind of minutiae that weave themselves into ever enlarging contexts. A trout stream points backward to geology and atmospherics, to history and evolution; it leads forward to insects and fish, to hydrology and botany, to literature and philosophy. Connections branch and rebranch in overlapping associations until finally, from the pattern of venation in a mayfly wing, you can reconstruct an entire watershed. In this regard, fly fishing is entirely self-explanatory, for by nature it revolves around on its own most revealing image—the riseform. The rise of trout to a drifting insect reverberates in expanding, concentric ripples, magnified iterations of a simple event that resonate outward to encompass more and more, remaining visible long after and far from the thing that made them. The rings of a rising trout eventually comprehend the entire river, yet no matter how large their compass, like all circles they never cease to invite an inference of the center.

The craft of angling is the catching of fish. But the art of angling is a receptiveness to these connections, the art of letting one thing lead to another until, if only locally and momentarily, you realize some small completeness. By no coincidence, this is the art of writing essays, as it is, I think, the art of living, for among these three occupations there seems to me no essential difference in degree or kind.

"One thing leading to another" is perhaps as good a description as any of the subject and method of this book. Its chapters, like the ripples of a riseform, trace the reverberations of a single circumstance, both outward to meanings and consequences, and inward to origins and sources. Over twenty years ago, I caught my first trout on a dry fly. Since then, I have been pleasantly haunted by the echoes of that event, now augmented and amplified in this place of unceasing seasons. This book is an attempt to make those echoes audible.

Looking back over these pages, I find that the effort has been framed by a few central questions, ones, I believe, that preoccupy many fishermen: What is the strange gravity of a trout stream? Why do we slow our cars and crane our necks at every bridge? What, exactly, are we looking for? What is it about rivers that draws us so irresistibly, and why does fly fishing seem to us such an aptly suited response? To fish the artificial fly is to make a deliberate decision about an approach and method; what does the choice signify? What urge propels it and what meanings are implied? There is always more to fishing than meets the eye, and often enough the invisible parts are the most compelling.

But most of all, this book is an attempt to discover points of fixity and pattern in our involvement with rivers and landscapes, with trout and fly fishing, as a way of plumbing their peculiar sustaining power. Most fishermen find better footing in the shifting forces of current than on what is called solid ground. Sea-legs come naturally; it's land-legs that are likely to prove troublesome. In a world that rolls ceaselessly underfoot, rocking and lurching like a subway car, I've found that the cork grip of a fly rod offers a pretty steady handhold—an unremarkable fact that becomes interesting only when, one day, you look up and ask just what the other end of that rod might be attached to. Though I can't prove a thing, I trust that it's something solid.

Faith and an open question, I suppose, is where most books, like most fishing trips, begin.

Corvallis, Oregon
1993

1

A Moveable Feast

The Ancient of Days forever is young,

Forever the scheme of Nature thrives;

I know a wind in purpose strong—

It spins against the way it drives.

—*Herman Melville, "The Conflict of Convictions"*

Above a ragged treeline, the thin curl of a waning moon lingers in the blue-black sky of five A.M. Tomorrow, the last sliver of light will vanish altogether, resetting the clock to some paradoxical beginning—a new moon (although there's nothing to see) and spring tides (on this, the first day of November). On the Pacific coast, gravity is a very serious business. The coupled forces of sun and moon breed exaggerated rhythms in the new tides. The ebb falls unusually low, baring the clam flats and shrinking the bay back to the broad canal of the riverbed. The flood runs hard and high, bearing schools of salmon that wiggle upriver in spermatozoic surges deep into the coastal mountains where they sow their own particular version of life. It's a pretty odd arrangement, even for nature.

Six miles above the head of tide, I drive slowly along the dark highway and look out the open window. A worn bearing in the trailer clicks like a casino wheel as I search for an opening in the roadside brush that marks the boat slide. The entrance is nearly overgrown, unused for almost half a year. On the third try, I at last square up the trailer to a shaggy opening in the undergrowth. The slide is an ad hoc, one-way trail to the river, down which a boat can, theoretically, be slipped into the water. It is substantially less graceful than the name implies. This one runs thirty rocky yards down a 20 percent grade, ending in a four-foot vertical drop, and cross-hatched along its length with thick whips of Himalaya vine and hard-tipped thorns. There's no mystery to the launch, which works just like it looks—you shove the boat stern-first down the slide and, grabbing hold of the bow rope, you ski down behind it over dirt and gravel, attempting in some puny way to influence the rate of descent. Once set in motion, the business takes on a life of its own with several conceivable outcomes, only one of which is good. This morning, it goes according to plan, and I skid almost to a standstill just as sixteen feet of McKenzie River driftboat teeters over the fulcrum of the bank and bounces lightly on the cushion of the river. I push off with an oar, and the boat chatters across a last submerged rock, into a weightless drift.

Ahead lies an apparently simple geometry—the salmon migrate upriver, the fisherman down, and somewhere along this thin ribbon of water, the opposing vectors converge. It's astonishing, though, how much more complicated the matter can become.

The salmon run is a moveable feast, predictably annual but with no better sense of timing than any other birth. Neither an exact point nor a specific interval, it is at best a distribution of statistical likelihoods around the nucleus of autumn. If the rains come, salmon—silvers and chinook—may enter the bay as early as August; if not, October may come and go without appreciable numbers of fish in the river. The last four years have been dry like this, and the movements of the salmon have become more indeterminate still. You can rely, really, only on two certainties: starting point and direction. From there, you either take up a vantage point and wait for the run to come to you, which is more reliable, or you try to hit a moving target, which is decidedly more interesting.

Despite appearances to the contrary, nature rarely operates in smooth continuities; or rather, it does so only in aggregate, over the long haul. In finer structures—from atomic quanta, to the convulsions of birth, to exploding stars—the universe changes in local abruptnesses punctuated by the dormancies of anticipation and aftermath. The salmon run is not a steady stream, but a succession of irregular spasms, and the fish congregate only intermittently through the river, in those certain places that offer temporary respite and a staging ground. Out in the bay, the salmon hold in deep holes and channels, where they are sought out in one of angling's more dismal spectacles.

Every autumn up and down the coast, hundreds and hundreds of boats, from tiny prams to sportfishers, work the estuary from daybreak to dusk, trolling when the tide runs, anchoring on the slack to cast or stillfish. They pack themselves together in frenetic and appalling densities that beggar specific description but generally resemble the other venues of psychotic consumerism here in the Disney empire. Most of the boats carry sonar gear, partly to read the depth and contour of the bottom, but mostly to find fish. A salmon passing beneath the vigilant eye of a transducer registers as a blip on a video screen that, just to be safe, emits an all-too-audible, exclamatory "ping!" When a school of salmon passes beneath the boats, the whole fleet pipes a calliope of digitized beeps that provides exactly the kind of circus-like ambiance that the whole scene so richly warrants.

I don't object to their methods, all the hardware and bait, but to their approach. The boaters watch screens rather than water and fish for LCD blips instead of salmon, oblivious to the noise, the diesel fumes, and the fantastic congestion of two-cycle outboards coughing blue smoke under the burden of too many baseball hats and Budweisers. And rippling beneath the skin of it all, like nitrogen in the blood, the distinct tingling hysteria of avarice. Even conscientious catch-and-release fishermen, if they're honest, will admit the difficulty of handling a big fish without a momentary, impulsive desire to possess it. Meat fishermen indulge this as a principle of being.

Among the boats, there's little room for a fly fisherman, but six miles farther down, the estuary opens out into a broad bay, and you can wade a shallow, hard-packed bottom that slopes gently to the deeper water of the channel. Salmon don't pause here; they just pass through, which means that most casts fall on empty water and you're fishing mainly for a species of coincidence. But comfortably distant from the prop wash and chaos of the meat-bucket trollers, the place is pretty much your own. No one else wants it.

Though I might come here once or twice a season, nothing about this fishing is really my style. The water demands big tackle—long, powerful rods with 9- or 10-weight lines (as much for casting distance and the wind as for the fish); big streamers; stout reels with lots of backing; and a high tolerance for repetition. For a while, after a summer and fall of precise, fussy trout fishing, there's pleasure in wading waist-deep and airing out long, targetless casts just for the change. But a few hours of bucking a steady right-hand wind, of staring into the glare, of forever tending loose coils of floating line that sieve out every kind of bay-crap imaginable—a few hours of this will use you up. Then, too, as a born midwesterner, whose first and most enduring concept of an ocean was 100,000 square miles of cornfields, I've never felt much at home around saltwater, and particularly these brackish bays. They seem strange, halfway places, zones of biological seething whose fertility overwhelms. The broadcast larvae of a billion invertebrates—bivalves, urchins, jellyfish, crustaceans—sluice around your legs in a hungry, primal bisque that doesn't know you from Adam. I'm not afraid of being drowned or devoured, but I am always aware of a remotely sinister feel about the place, as though something is perpetually on the edge of happening. In short, it gives me the creeps.

Fishing the bay is all business; it exists only for the moments of catching, which are as spectacular as they are rare. Set the hook in a fresh silver salmon, and it will tailwalk on 100 feet of line before you can swallow hard. A big chinook, bright as a full moon, can peel you like an egg. After the monotonous iteration of casting, the instant of sudden connection to some enormous, unseen vitality borders on religious experience and happens about as often—the kind of thing, as the grade-school nuns used to threaten, that will "make a believer out of you," as though believing was a fate to steer clear of.

But I come mainly for a different kind of revelation. Particularly in years when the run is strong, there are times when the bay is alive with salmon, breaking the water like dolphins in rolling arcs and reckless, vertical leaps. If you pick out a piece of water, accustom your eyes to it, and watch a while, fish are almost continually visible, sometimes in twos and threes, sometimes dozens at once. Some vantage points, though, are better than others. Up the bay about a mile from the hard-bottom flats, the road climbs a small rise that marks a weathered rock outcrop overlooking the water. If you stand on the edge of this low bluff and face up the bay, you can step left or right, or back a little, adjusting your position until you locate a certain, specific point of view. This particular angle of vision screens out all the houses and highways, the rotting log pilings, the buoys and powerlines, and extinguishes from the landscape every evidence of human influence. Laid out before you are only the low coastal mountains shagged in cedar and fir, the windchop glittering in the sun, and the curves of leaping salmon, retracing an ancestral pattern 40,000 years old. Strings of geese pass overhead, pushed south by the tilting earth just as packs of salmon are drawn upriver by the moon. Watching, you get some dim idea of how it all used to be, some small glimpse from the edge of winter at a world before the fall. It may be, perhaps, no more than a trick of perspective, of selection and exclusion, of lines and angles. But it is no less either. In the end, imagination is a tactic of geometry.

The river is a flux, the salmon a counterflux. To fish the run is to share this paradoxical trajectory, moving at once forward to a conclusion and backward toward sources. Fish and fishermen both work upstream, pursuing ends but oriented toward beginnings, winnowing the extraneous to converge on essentials. Ten centuries ago, in the salmon camps of the Tillamook, Coquille, and Umpqua tribes, the talk would have seemed familiar to a fisherman today, the same matters he might speak of, in the same tones of voice. There would be apprehension if the run was late or weak, restlessness if the fish arrived but not the rains to draw them upriver to the spawning grounds. Dark salmon, rolling in tidewater and ripe with eggs, could not ascend the river; should urgency force them to dig redds in the silt, fish and fishermen would suffer disaster. But if the run were strong, it would be met with gratitude and gathered like a blessing. To those who pay attention, the coming of the salmon has as much to do with a world view as anything, with a cosmos in or out of kilter.

This, I suppose, as far as I can explain it, is the reason I've coaxed myself out of bed long before dawn, managed just enough coffee to simulate consciousness, and driven in a half-sleep for over an hour to arrive at the river before sunrise. The salmon run is a confluence of origins and eventualities when, for a moment, life wraps round and touches its own tail. The countercurrents of river and fish, of beginnings and endings, of ancient days and new ones, are briefly contiguous. Still at sea, the salmon sense home rivers on the faintest dilution of fresh water and know its significance with the certainty of instinct. But a fisherman must work to unravel the meaning, and finally his fishing is only an argument, a studied drawing of inferences about undisclosed things.

The boat slips quietly downriver, and the sense of dislocation from the present, managed on the bay only by a discreet selection of vantage points, comes more easily here. Thick growth along the banks insulates the river from whatever lies beyond. On much of this six-mile drift, the land slopes too steeply for farms or houses and, at this time of year, there's little chance of seeing another fisherman. The lack of rain has kept the river low, and the shallow water is irksome to navigate. The boat scrapes against barely submerged boulders, rattles and bangs down the inclines of shallow riffles. At the shoals I'll have to get out and drag it over. More conscientious fishermen refuse to subject their boats to the abuse, feeling each gouge on the bottom or chine like a nick in the soul. I don't care that much, having always bought used boats for the same reason I buy used cars—they free up your attention for more important things.

At the end of a long glide, just as the water breaks over a lip of rocks and drops into a riffle, I see the first few fish—three wide mounds of water in the tailout. They could be boulders, except that they sway from side to side. In response to some cue, each mound splits in perfect halves, like a dividing chromosome. Six salmon, three pairs. Watching them, I've let the boat drift too close and quickly try to stall the drift. An oar crabs the shallow bottom and rattles lightly in the oarlock—a faint tick of metal-on-metal that must reverberate underwater like a train wreck. The six fish bolt upriver in an instant, never breaking the surface but pushing big bow waves ahead of them like cartoon torpedoes. One fish passes near enough for a good look, and I see that it is, or was, a silver.

The current angles toward the middle of the river and carries the boat over three redds in a foot of water, spaced uniformly across the streambed. Fifteen feet below them, I drop the anchor and wait, not to fish, but to watch. In time, maybe two minutes, maybe twenty, the fish will return, warily at first, their approach a taut and skittish vacillation between two irreconcilable instincts. They edge cautiously down the glide from deeper water, only to withdraw when they catch sight of me. Then again, this time closer. And in the end, the pull of the redds proves an irresistible gravity, and the impulse to protect them overrules all others. The boat fades into the background and becomes for them no more than some unremembered fixture of the river. The fish drift back and settle in. Fresh water and spawning have tarnished the once lustrous silver bodies to an ashy gray, and the salmon cut conspicuous silhouettes on the sand-colored bottom. The mates converge, each pair seeming for a while a single fish, motionless except for flaring gills and the slow sweep of tails. They begin circling the redds, nose to tail, abruptly breaking off and facing into the current, six streaks in parallel, a Khien hexagram suspended in water as transparent as air. The salmon move gracefully, are perhaps even beautiful, but what holds you to the spot is their perfect visibility. The fish you can believe; it's the fact of your seeing them that seems incredible.

Every year, the spectacle of the run prompts a spot on the five-o'clock news (again at eleven) with footage of spawning salmon and the kind of hushed voiceover usually reserved for golf tournaments: "Using her tail, the female fans a nest in the gravel where the eggs will be deposited, while the male waits nearby, guarding the nest and challenging rivals." The description is accurate in the usual soundbite sort of way, glimpsing only a little scenery where there is in fact a landscape. A ten-pound silver salmon will "fan a nest in the gravel" by digging out bushels of rocks the size of Texas grapefruit. The redd of a thirty-five-pound hen chinook looks like the excavation for a bridge piling; at low water it becomes a navigational hazard. The males do in fact devote substantial energy to "challenging rivals"—by ramming them broadside in explosive bursts of speed, or by seizing an offending tail in a scythe-like kype full of teeth, grown just for the occasion, and shaking an adversary like a terrier with a rat. Considering the alternatives, between dying on the one hand and having sex and dying on the other, the violence makes a certain sense from the salmon's point of view, and at times seems contested in the consciousness of precisely this finality.

More often, though, the dynamics are ritualized, four or five fish holding in tense, territorial geometries. Position, spacing, and attitude all communicate significance, and any small change or disturbance in the lines of force provokes an anxious shifting of the entire configuration, until it finally readjusts to a new, equally temporary, equilibrium of dominance and submission. The details are perfectly inscrutable, like non-combative displays of all kinds. A pair of male fence lizards face off and with arched necks flash electric blue dewlaps at one another while a female looks on. Abruptly, somehow, the thing is decided, and one of the males skitters off. In the frantic dance of sharp-tailed grouse, the solemn croaking of bullfrogs, the ionized body-language of a Saturday-night bar, bloodless battles are fought, winners and losers determined through secret, conspecific meanings. It's an insider's game, and finally who wins is far less interesting than the way in which victory is suddenly and simply understood by all involved.

I lift the anchor, and the boat slides downriver. Fishing these spawners holds little appeal. I'd like to say that I pass them up out of some high moral principle, some refusal to exploit their weakness. But this wouldn't be entirely true. When I first moved to Oregon from Virginia, I left behind the small brook trout of the Blue Ridge and found the biggest fish I'd ever seen in my life. The very sight of them induced a consuming, if temporary, big-game psychosis. I fished for any salmon I could find, which were usually dark ones, and eventually caught enough of them (it didn't take many) to recognize that there was no sport in their sluggish, preoccupied resistance. I began to feel a little guilty about it. For a couple of reasons, I distinctly recall the last dark fish I ever deliberately cast to, a beast of a salmon hugging the river bottom in a swift, narrow chute along the bank. The fish hit a Glo-Bug on the first cast, and lumbered wearily up the run into a large elliptical pool fed by a low falls at the head. Then, in one of the more craven acts of my angling life, I stepped into the tail-out, and trapped the fish in the pool. This, more than anything subsequent, sealed the matter.

Unwilling to jump the falls, though it easily could have, and terrified of approaching me, the salmon just circled the smooth pool of naked bedrock—no deadfalls to foul the line, no boulders to snag the leader, no place to go. For all practical purposes, I was playing the fish in a giant gravy boat; given time, I could have landed it on a spool of fly-tying thread. The salmon swam back and forth across the pool in arcs of gradually diminishing radius, and at the end of fifteen minutes a hen chinook lay in the shallows at my feet. I had to use both hands to tail the largest fish I'd ever taken, on a fly or otherwise. At the time I judged the fish to be a shade under forty pounds; big salmon I've seen since then have done nothing to lower that estimate. Almost at once, the tawdriness of the whole episode flashed on me, and I released the fish with no sense of achievement, but only the same mixture of shame and profound regret one sometimes feels after "winning" a protracted and particularly bitter domestic argument.

Occasionally, though, a fresh fish swims among the dark spawners. You need patience to find one and a certain stealth to approach within casting range, and at such times it is never clearer that sight-fishing to large fish, whether tarpon or bonefish, steelhead or salmon, is really a species of hunting. Around mid-morning, I see the only bright salmon of the day, a streak of pewter among eight or ten other fish, some nearly black, others the color of old bricks. The pod drifts, and disperses, and reforms in a random amoeba-like streaming, always a coherence but never quite a shape. The general movement of the school is confined to a riffle about thirty feet square, a portion of which lies in the shade on the far bank.

Other fish may be holding in the shadows; I can't tell, but know it's wise to make the assumption. By nature, a river deceives. What you can observe of it—the flux, drift, motion, the incessant fact of passing—tempts you to mistake the current for the river, and so see only direction where there is indirection as well. A river leads a double life in which the visible is an index to the invisible. What appears to be a school of spawning salmon is in fact a nearly self-contained ecosystem. Unseen in the slipstream below the shifting pod of fish, an entourage has assembled—resident trout, jacks, sea-run cutthroats, a large coastal variety of sculpin, crayfish, smolts, an occasional steelhead, and once in a while, a fly fisherman. Every opportunist, freeloader, and hanger-on in the river finds something in the wake of the salmon—slack current to rest in, eggs that drift from the beds, nymphs and crustaceans dislodged by the ceaseless digging of redds. During the run, the river contracts to local densities of activity, comet-shaped gradients of life that for a brief duration put the whole system on a perceivable scale. That this enormous vitality draws you to it, as it draws other things, seems hardly an accident.

The bright fish I've spotted holds near the center of the school. I poke through my fly boxes and finally choose a #10 Skykomish Sunrise, more on whim than anything, since I've determined that, most of the time, the specific pattern is less significant than color, color less important than size, and size almost immaterial anyway. The salmon act on whims of their own, and fishing for them is largely a matter of catching them in the right humor. Casting upstream, as though nymphing to trout, I let the fly sink and roll down to the fish, throwing slack or tightening the line to guide the drift and avoid snagging a dark spawner. The bright body of the fly, intermittently visible through the water, helps me keep track of things. As it tumbles across the bottom, the pod of fish splits in perfect synchrony as though repelled by some invisible field, and the fly drifts down an empty aisle. The fish are neither spooked nor interested, and cast after cast produces nothing but a wide swath in the school. I think of seasons past, and it is just as I remember—the salmon run as a moveable feast, my fishing as a moveable famine.

I change flies, and on the first cast a #12 Silver Hilton stops abruptly halfway through the riffle. Braced for resistance, I lean back hard. The rod bends sharply, then recoils, and a small trout-shaped projectile half-a-foot long, clinging to a Silver Hilton, skims past my right ear—a "launcher" in local parlance, a small fish with a great misfortune that trips the hair-trigger of anticipation and spends a confusing moment airborne. I release it, and when I look back to the riffle, the one bright salmon in the bunch has vanished.

At the edge of the school a few jack salmon swim cautiously, alert to the main chance, but aware of their own vulnerability. The jacks are an evolutionary adaptation of the species, sexually precocious males that spend only a year at sea rather than the customary three or four. For the most part, they tag along with the run as an emergency measure, ready to reproduce but rarely getting the chance when larger adult males are about. But should a female arrive unmated, the jacks will ensure that the eggs are fertilized. Apparently, they succeed just often enough. Roughly the same proportion of each year's brood return as jacks, and their abundance or scarcity in a given year offers some indication of the strength of the adult run a few seasons down the road, when the rest of the year-class returns from a full term at sea.

In this age of "enhanced fisheries," when most salmon are reared in hatcheries and tended like livestock, jacks have become not only irrelevant, but biologically objectionable. A fish that successfully mates may pass along its genes for jackhood, and in the governing management strategy, this is bad business. Male offspring that might mature to full-sized adults with a different paternity—and thus constitute a more "commercially viable return on investment" when the "resource" is "harvested"—reenter the river instead as meager jacks themselves. Such is the calculus of the modern fish farm, which seeks to rid the run of these genetic undesirables by placing generous limits on them—ten per day in Oregon—a policy that has met with as little result as the practice of stocking itself. The number of jacks is decreasing, but only because the runs themselves are diminishing, and many rivers are in serious trouble. Already we are alarmingly close to the day when wild fish will be inadvertent, wandering anomalies, scratching out a living like feral hogs.

Another mile and the river horseshoes back from the old highway into a woods of Douglas fir, hemlock, cedar, and vinemaple. The most beautiful section of the drift begins here, and for a time I put up the oars, sit on the flydeck, and watch the river, partly for salmon, but mostly for itself. In the smooth glides, every detail on the bottom rises in relief. The bed of cobbles, crayfish with waving claws, swirling patches of sand, sunken trees, and mosaics of waterlogged leaves, all pass beneath you in an endless, hypnotic succession. Shallows drop suddenly into inky pools. Boulders loom up from an unseen bottom to touch the surface, and then disappear. Underwater canyons wind through broken ledgerock cliffs. Here and there, the river bottom is scoured to clean bedrock, vast rippled sheets of it fractured into blocks that are pitted and pocked with circular, foot-deep craters. The boat drifts above it all in effortless silence, like a hot-air balloon. The sense of remoteness is absolute. Staring overboard with no other reference point but the river, you can easily persuade yourself that the boat is motionless and the river slipping backward beneath you.

In a few places, the streambed shelves off into black-bottomed pools where silt has settled out in the slow currents. During the run, salmon congregate in this deep water, and at morning and evening when the light is low, they roll and leap incessantly, clearing the surface in long flat arcs and slapping back down, or churning the water in deep boils that leave slowly dissolving whirlpools. The behavior is common among all anadromous fishes, though no more comprehensible for that. Explanations, however, abound. Fishermen, like the rest of humankind, will talk relentlessly and authoritatively about what they understand least. I've been told, to take but a sample, that salmon roll because they are trying to shake loose eggs from the skeins; because the water is too warm; because they are gulping air; because they are trying to rid themselves of sea lice and parasites; because they don't like fresh water (it kills them, as you can plainly see); and simply because they're horny—an explanation with at least the ring of truth. There are those who mourn the passing of the American rural culture, and every summer the Appalachian and Smokey Mountains swarm with well-scrubbed boys and girls from tony New England colleges, cruising the backroads in vans full of sound gear, taping oral folk histories. They ought to come west. Few can match the Pacific salmon fisherman for picturesque absurdities.

These deep pools may be classic salmon water, but they can't really be fished in the classic fashion, if such a term describes the tedious double-hauling of high-density or lead-core shooting heads on eighty-foot casts. The river for the most part is too small, and the pools offer too little current to animate a fly properly. On holes with steep banks and deep water, I'll make a pass through with a floating line and a small, heavily dressed fly, casting to the bank and retrieving in short twitches. When that fails, and it usually does, I resort to a sinking line and a larger pattern, and begin the kind of laborious blind-dredging that has earned fly fishing for Pacific salmon the half-deserved reputation as a sport for iron wills and soft brains.

Small wavelets slap the boat bottom as it rides a little tongue of current into the head of the pool. Though it is past midday, a salmon rolls in the shade of alder limbs arching over the water. In the heart or mind or wherever essences reside, I am a trout fisherman, which means among other things that any surface disturbance made by a fish, for whatever reason, automatically registers on the consciousness as a "rise." It is an instinctual association against which all knowledge, better judgment, and experience are helpless, and when the salmon breaks the water, I row over and begin covering it with expectant, pointless casts. Years of humoring this particular delusion have yielded exactly two salmon, neither of which in all likelihood had actually rolled, but just happened to be in the vicinity of a fish that did. Today does not bring a third.

The bank has promising depth here, though, and I continue slowly along it, placing casts at rhythmic two-foot intervals, thinking of other things. Near the tail of the pool, the water behind the fly billows gently with the quick pass of a fish. But no grab. A hard roll cast returns the fly to the still-dissipating ripple. A few fast strips of line and the surface swirls again, this time more violently, but with no more definitive result. Dropping the fly back a third time, I let it sink for perhaps half a minute and inch it back, flicking the rod tip now and again to send a tight shiver down the line. As the fly approaches the boat, I can see the salmon following a foot behind, matching the erratic retrieve precisely, advancing when the fly does, pausing when I pause, maintaining a scrupulous distance. Only a rod-length away the fish stops, a soot-colored male coho of perhaps six pounds. It holds just beneath the surface, canted slightly upward, staring past me with an eye fixed severely on something remote. This dark eye and the fiercely hooked kype remind me of a bird of prey.

For all that is magnificent about the salmon—the clean, taut hydrodynamic lines; the thick muscling; the glints of blue, green, and indigo flashing from a silver skin—for all these, it seems strange that the eye and kype should be the features that haunt. Something must inhere in them, for they haunted the past as well, recurring again and again, almost obsessively, in carved and painted images of the Klickitat, Tlingit, and Haida, as though these features alone expressed some deep essence of the animal.

The salmon turns and disappears downward. But the eye and the kype linger in afterimage, abstracted halos of life's determination for itself. It seems to me no accident that salmon flesh and salmon spawn are precisely the same color, as though the animal reconstitutes its very substance into another generation. But here and now, in the middle of the run, the continuity is only an inference, an assumption, a conjecture to be believed in. What is visible is only life leaking from the salmon in the increments of a million eggs, and this is the most compelling and lasting impression of the run, not of poised vitality, but of dying. The gradual darkening of fish in fresh water is a triumph of fertility and the intimation of doom. Sex and death are forever linked, I suppose, but never so tangibly and unequivocally as in the salmon. Even now, the first fish are spawned out and dead, washed by the current into calm water and visible on the river bottom. Some are ringed with scavenging crayfish, others encrusted with the cases of caddis flies that will themselves be food for smolts and turn carrion back into salmon. This seems a long way off, though.

In a rain forest or a drop of pond water, we are accustomed to the spectacle of extravagant potency. But death is exactly as profligate as life, and when more of the run arrives and spawns, the gravel bars and shoals will be strewn with dead fish, their dried skins shrunken tightly over ribs like the caved-in fuselages of things that once flew. The odor of decay hovers above the river, the acrid, musty, ammoniac smell of an old horsehair sofa stained with cat piss. When the first heavy rain of winter comes, raising the water to twice its height before subsiding, the flaccid carcasses of salmon will hang twisted and draped from bankside limbs in grotesque postures, like a Dali painting. Still later, there are only bones. The hollow-eyed skulls with long, beaked jaws scarcely resemble the living animal at all. They seem strange and ancient, distantly reptilian or avian, like the fossil of an *Archaeopteryx* I once saw, perfectly preserved down to the finest imprint of its scale-like feathers.

If you fish much during the run, what strikes you most is how slowly this all occurs. Salmon do not spawn and drop dead. They weaken by degrees. Many fall victim to a debilitating, cottony fungus that tatters the fins and tail, and eventually covers the body in gauzy patches. A ragged fish may hang on well into winter, ghosting through the river and looking as purposeless as in fact it is—"a shroud in a gutter," Ted Hughes writes, "a death-in-life." The first January I spent in Oregon, wading this same river for winter steelhead, I half glimpsed through the riffled water an enormous mottled form that would not resolve itself into a familiar object. It moved downstream toward me with the thick-bodied sluggishness of a moray eel. I edged backward against the bank, keeping a close eye on it, not quite panicked but distinctly uneasy. It turned and followed. At the moment I recognized it as an exhausted, rotting salmon, the fish slid its length along my shin, and the contact reverberated in an involuntary full-body shiver. After that, I couldn't seem to get warm again, and left. Death underwrites life, I know, but when it comes right up and brushes your leg, all that seems somehow unconsoling.

If we share anything with the past it is a sense of the violence in nature. The Puritans looked at a wild New World and saw the abode of the devil, and they battled it with a ferocity that equaled the savageness of their perception. Now, having distanced ourselves from the wilderness, we view it through an imperturbable Darwinism, an indifferent survival-of-the-fittest. But all that we've really done is alter the terms. Dismissing the moral repercussions of struggle, we have only tamed ourselves. Nature remains a place of violent death. And in a world of quick, predatory kills, of fangs and claws and coils, the slow decay of the salmon seems anomalous, and eerily human.

A sharp west wind rises, blowing upstream and bringing with it a sheet of gray clouds. Caught in the shear of opposing currents, the boat is almost motionless. I have to row to make any headway.

The river bends back to the highway and to the sound of log haulers downshifting on a switchback grade. There are no more salmon to be seen. When a small island eventually appears ahead, I pull to the right of the river and skid over a sandy shoal, down a tight channel barely wide enough for the boat. Halfway down at the pull-out point, I tie the bow-line to a willow. The truck is waiting, shuttled down by arrangement. I dig the spare keys from my pocket and, twisting around in the seat, looking over my shoulder to back the trailer to the river's edge, I see on the rear window the first streaks of the first winter rain.

2

Anchors

Some have said they have felt a boat shudder before she struck a rock, or cry when she beached and the surf poured into her. This is not mysticism, but identification; man, building this greatest and most personal of all tools, has in turn received a boat-shaped mind, and the boat a man-shaped soul.

—*John Steinbeck,* The Log from the Sea of Cortez

To locate yourself in new territory and lay some claim more consequential than a mailing address, I believe you must seek out what could be called its "sense of place," that particular weave of relationships among plants, animals, people, landscape, ideas, and history that flourishes more or less uniquely under local circumstance. I know of only one way to go about the search—take up a single thread of the fabric, follow it, and just let one thing lead to another. If you fish, you already have the advantage of a starting point, so when I dropped anchor in Oregon ten years ago, I bought a new fly rod, tied up some local patterns, and went looking for steelhead.

Above all other fish, steelhead were to me the most intriguing natives of the Northwest. They defined its angling identity. Even though from northern California to Alaska, there were thousands, perhaps tens of thousands of miles of steelhead water, my imagination returned always to a few rivers—the North Umpqua, the Deschutes, the Rogue. Steelhead could be found elsewhere, but Oregon was steelhead country. That first winter, I fished eagerly, often, and in deep ignorance. When the run at last tailed off in March, I had hooked exactly four steelhead and landed two of them. There are advantages to being self-taught; the quality of instruction is not one of them.

The summer steelhead, I'd heard, came more readily to the fly. But when summer came, I found myself too absorbed in trout fishing to bother, and the steelhead season passed without a single trip. During the warm months I nevertheless incubated little plans for the upcoming winter, read up on the subject, tended pet theories, tied new flies. The second winter went a bit better than the first, and the next year a bit better yet. Eventually, I logged enough river time and caught just enough steelhead to realize that I had neither a taste nor an aptitude for it, though I never determined which of these was a cause, which an effect. The fishing cooled of its own accord, trips tapered off to four or five a year, and I now find myself in the heart of steelhead country, lamely explaining why I fish them so seldom.

In fact, I raise the subject at all less for itself than for what the fish unexpectedly led me to. The first steelhead trip, and many thereafter, were undertaken with a partner, also new to Oregon, in a borrowed McKenzie River driftboat—a shameful, wooden disaster of archaic design, dryrotted in a few vital areas, with oversized oars. It seemed to float by accident. Neither of us knew much about running it, though, and for many seasons it functioned better as a boat than we did as boatmen. Its virtues on the water and its fittedness to a landscape of rivers were instantly apparent to me. Driftboats belonged in the place, and to know them, I felt, would be to understand something of importance. If you approach it properly, fishing has no endpoints, only new points of departure. I had sought out wild steelhead as an embodiment of some native idea, some spirit that made the place itself. The pursuit led, eventually and obliquely, to the discovery of a second indigenous form. From that moment on, steelhead and driftboats have been inseparably linked in my imagination.

Their connection goes beyond the coincidence of private experience; the two share deeper affinities. Like steelhead, driftboats are anadromous, descended from the double-ended ocean dories that were launched through the breakers and rowed out to meet the incoming salmon. The lineage extends still further back, possibly through the river batteaux, to the banks dories of the North Atlantic cod fishery. In the Northwest, the design idea migrated up the McKenzie River and spawned. Becoming smaller and more maneuverable, the boats adapted to survive in the swift, churning currents and bouldered drops of white-water rivers. They evolved at last into a separate race altogether, like the steelhead that long ago ascended prehistoric rivers, lingering there to become strains of resident rainbows that never again looked seaward. In recent times, both the fish and the boats have been transplanted to other regions, but they remain authentically native forms, quick and stream-lined, thriving in rough water through slipperiness and cunning rather than raw strength. Down to the finest detail, they are perfectly suited to their regional habitat.

The evolutionary adaptations of the driftboat are ingenious. They are unusually beamy craft, with wide, flat bottoms and high, flaring sides that produce a remarkable stability. A driftboat will tolerate an angle of heel that would capsize most small boats; you can stand on the gunnel without tipping one over. Built for buoyancy and shallow draught, the hull draws less than six inches of water and will slip over the shallowest flats. Stem and transom are sharply angled. From stem to stern, the bottom is not flat but severely rockered, curved fore and aft, and the combination of broad beam and rocker puts the center of gravity almost at the oarsman's feet. A well-made boat answers the oarsman's lightest touch; it will turn, stop, pivot, and deftly pick its way through the obstacle course of a rocky rapids with astonishingly little effort.

Like steelhead, a driftboat is the perfect union of form and function, all beauty and business, and one of the most honest things on the planet. Few other craft will perform the same function, and none with such elegance. A whitewater raft will transport you downriver, but it is sluggish and clumsy, handling precisely like what it is—an ungainly bag of gas. But the hull of a driftboat is geometric grace, a curvature in space defined by smooth, arced planes that intersect like the vault of a cathedral. It holds no hint of ugliness. A driftboat has a simplicity, a clearness of vision, and a sense of purpose so absolute that it might have sprung from the uncluttered heart of a Shaker.

Were it possible to separate a river into the physical components of water and current, to divide the liquid from the flux it expresses, the water would settle into a formless calm. But the current would be shaped like a fish, or the wing of a bird, or a driftboat—things not merely streamlined but streamlike. They are formed to slip with a minimum of disturbance through worlds where the most compelling fact of existence is friction. This, I think, is one of the deep attractions of driftboats. They seem to be *on* the water rather than in it, propelled by the flow but somehow above it. The flat, stable bottom is as perfect an observation deck as it is a fishing platform, and I've never drifted with anyone who did not become completely absorbed in watching the landscape glide by. Moving but motionless, you come to feel invisible and weightless, slipping silently past deer, otter, herons, and fish, so that a driftboat now seems to me less a way of traveling a river than a way of inhabiting it.

There's one last thing, and perhaps the most important one. Most small boats are designed to hold a steady course, to oppose crosswinds and currents that would deflect them from the line of travel. To this end, they are built with keels that are aligned on the hull like a compass needle and use the resistance of the water itself to maintain a steady bearing. Keels are inertial, an argument for the way things are; they enforce constancy and direction, which is precisely their value. But the flat bottom of a driftboat is keelless, offering nothing to hinder transverse motion. It rides the uppermost sheet of water and shunts the current aside, slipping obliquely over the surface and outwitting the flux. A driftboat invites the sidelong and tangential, offering above all else an overwhelming sense of frictionlessness as the ordinary drift of things slides past.

Keellessness is a reversal that inspires a distinct kind of navigation. Maneuvering a boat on moving water requires resistance; some force of push or pull is necessary to steer a course. Most craft achieve steerageway by traveling faster than the current, keeping always a step ahead of the river. This kind of boat-handling takes alertness, quick thinking, and instinctive reactions. But steerage velocity is relative, and you control a driftboat by going slower than the current instead of faster. You face downriver, but like a steelhead, your navigational orientation is upstream. Without a keel, the boat pivots and swivels in an instant, traverses the river from side to side, and holds against the flow, not by resisting it but by offering as little resistance as possible. You don't try to outrun the river; you gradually lower yourself down it, moving not with the speed of reflex but of reflection.

In the right water, a little trick can be worked that never fails to confound the first-timer. Where the river runs swiftly over shallow bedrock, a line of standing waves will develop. If they are spaced just right, you can trap the boat in a trough between two crests. Though the water rolls and swells on all sides, the waveform remains stationary, and the boats sits calmly amid the turbulence in apparent defiance of some law. You occupy a place within a place, holding in the flux, anchored by the water itself. And you see the river with new eyes.

To forgo a keel is not to forsake direction but to invite a kind of suspension, one that multiplies the dimensions and degrees of freedom in which you move. You can pursue a sense of place in the particulars of landscape, but you ground that sense, I think, in your own vision. I first sought out steelhead as an incarnation of native form, some key to the lay of the land. One thing led to another, and I discovered in driftboats a second indigenous idea, a way of exploring the first that in time became anchored to a way of seeing. Still later I would learn that you don't even need the boat, that the anchor alone is sufficient.

3

Foxes and Hedgehogs

Winter is icummen in,

Lhude sing Goddamm . . .

—Ezra Pound, "Ancient Music"

It has always been the business of philosophy to parse the world, and in a fragment of an ancient poem, Archilocus of Paros splits it this way: "The fox knows many things," he writes, "but the hedgehog knows one big thing." The fox meets life with diversity and eclecticism. He is skeptical and adaptive, resourceful and canny, tolerant of the ambiguities of existence, an ironist. The hedgehog, on the other hand, is a creature of system, his view of life resolutely informed by some elemental faith. He is preeminently a believer, an inflexible enthusiast trusting to the long haul. In fishing, Charles Cotton, Frederic Halford, and Roderick Haig-Brown are hedgehogs. Ray Bergman, Lee Wulff, and A. J. McClane are its foxes.

Of anglers more generally, salmon and steelhead fishermen are inclined to be hedgehogs. They know the one big thing, whatever you wish to call it—an unyielding devotion to purpose, the righteousness of a calling, a preternatural faith in their own spiritual invulnerability. In hunting anadromous species, finesse is the first casualty. Tom McGuane once argued that the only requirements for steelhead fishing were a big arm and a room temperature IQ. There's something to this, though I suspect the matter of the arm is negotiable. The fishing calls for brute determination stoked by a faith so deep that it can't be told from instinct—a disposition perfectly suited to the fish themselves, fixed single-mindedly upon their own insistencies. They too know the one big thing.

The trout fisherman, however, is a fox, a tactician and strategist with a deference to contingencies and one eye perpetually over his shoulder. He improvises, ad libs, thinks on his feet.

If nothing else, look at their fly boxes. A steelhead angler might stock half-a-dozen patterns, and among these just one or two basic styles, varied a little in size and color. This is about as far as he's willing to compromise; that his boxes are filled to even this extent is mainly an acknowledgment that some flies will be lost to snags and, occasionally, fish. But if he makes enough casts and preserves his concentration—if he believes—he'll gain his reward.

The trout fisherman takes no chances. Dry flies, nymphs, floating nymphs, emergers, huge streamers and tiny midges, crustacean imitations, terrestrials, attractors—his fly boxes bristle with alternatives and backups, indemnities against an inconstant world. His approach is recursive, his fishing vest a succession of Plan Bs in which there's always an alternative, always something to fall back on.

Both types of fishermen will have their days, but their differences underscore the particular satisfaction I find in fishing trout during the winter, overwhelmingly the season of the hedgehog. It has about it the feeling of fishing posted water. Though not illegal, it holds out the pleasures of illicitness. Stripped of the sheltering particulars of summer, the landscape contracts to a hard limit. It's not barren, but it is empty except for you, a peeping Izaak who earns his furtive looks with a vicious windburn and a frozen ass. To catch a river unguarded is less a matter of where to look than of when, and so while other fishermen have secret places, I have a secret time.

Fishing in general has always seemed to me a form of subversion anyway. In a world that insists upon "means" and "ends," that dooms every path to a destination, fishing elides the categories and so slips the distinction altogether. You become engaged in the nonterminal, participial indefiniteness of "going fishing." It exists wholly for its own sake, productive (at least in the late-twentieth-century sense of the term) of absolutely nothing. Measured against the ledger-sheet sensibility, corporate or Calvinist, it is a form of anarchy, and that the legions of bottom-liners haven't yet sniffed it out as something dangerous baffles me a little. To go fishing is essentially functionless, though that's not at all the same thing as saying it is without purpose.

Casting flies for trout in winter is perhaps the most subversive of all. It cuts deeply against the grain, and the sense of inversion is profound and wholesale. Everything about winter fishing argues for its opposite. In summer, a trout stream is nothing less than a form of gravity, drawing all things to itself in a brilliant convergence of luminous currents and sunlight, translucent-winged mayflies, and the glittering rings of rising trout. It takes energy only to resist. The thrust of winter, though, is centrifugal, pushing things outward, driving them underground or driving them out. Merely getting a purchase against this kind of inertia requires effort; making any progress toward the center takes a will with superior traction.

The gear is of little help; it is built by summer, rigged for seduction rather than struggle, its employment a slender insinuation into the ways of the river. A looping fly line transcribes the contour of a breeze. Feathers and fur take the shape of an afternoon hatch. A fly rod curves with the trajectory of a June twilight. Each implies the other. But on a raw winter day, the tackle in the trunk seems far less substantial than it did six months ago, not so much inadequate as insufficiently material for what's ahead, and you wonder if maybe you made a mistake. Everything—the weather, the water, the fish, the absurdly tiny dry flies in a brittle plastic box, your own better judgment, all argue against your being there. But somehow there you are, urging private folly against prevailing wisdom, leaving others to wonder whether you know a little more or a little less than they do. Which is precisely the case.

The place I go to fish winter trout is not, oddly enough, in the comparatively warm valley lowlands or temperate coastal mountains, but 150 miles inland and 3,500 feet up the east slope of the Cascade range, often enough the upper limit of unfrozen water at this outer boundary of the year. Getting there means crossing two passes, and although not high ones by the benchmark of the Rockies—a bit below 5,000 feet—the sense of altitude is differential rather than absolute. My house sits on land 250 feet above sea level; the passes are twenty times that elevation. Just east of Sweet Home, the highway begins to climb, following the South Fork of the Santiam River that has gouged a narrow way through steep stands of Douglas fir and tangled branches of vinemaple that clatter emptily in the chill. Higher up, near Tombstone Pass, the last dampness of the maritime air is wrung out as snow from gray masses of clouds that pile up against the Pacific Crest. "Traction Devices," you are repeatedly informed, "Are Required," and the roadside is piled high with coarse volcanic cinder that was spread on the slippery grades. In summer, the highway is a string of summer vacationers piloting every sort of recreational land-barge imaginable. In winter, they are replaced by an endless injection-molded convoy of skiers; in my rearview mirror, their roof-racked cars look like cops.

Beyond the last pass the narrow highway hugs the flank of a mountain, and far below, Suttle Lake is a brief and precipitous miscalculation to the right. The flatter country beyond is the arid western fringe of an expanse of high desert that extends, more or less, to the far side of Idaho. The Douglas fir give way to Ponderosa pine and sagebrush, a few tentative stands of aspen, some white fir, and, wherever there is water, the tall spires of tamarack. Ahead is Black Butte, a 6,000-foot cinder cone, that long ago burped itself into existence and blocked a system of small watercourses. These now follow a prehistoric bed beneath the butte and percolate through the north edge of its base as the Metolius River—one of the worst-kept secrets in Oregon.

I've been told that the Metolius is the state's most heavily fished river, according to one of those inches-of-fish-per-rod-per-acre-per-day accountings that so precisely fail to convey anything worth knowing. But by the truer calculus of experience, I can attest that the stream stays in a constant casting lather from June to August; like any fisherman even mildly mindful of his sanity, I avoid the place in the summer. The upper river is strewn with campgrounds filled all season long with a chaos of mountain bikes, frisbees, and fly rods, amid the incessant low-level gargle of concealed RV generators. Fleeing the wrack and sputum of L.A., many of these folks have traveled north up Interstate 5 from planet California, and the antipathy that Oregonians (at least some of them) bear for Californians is the stuff of legend in this part of the world. It's less a rivalry than the sense of resentment borne by the invaded, whose homeland has suddenly become a consumable commodity—one of the richer ironies of living in a place whose economic existence is already underwritten by extractive industries. I can't say that I share the general enmity, but it is a matter of public record, the legacy of a former governor whose open invitation to visitors conveyed the barely disguised subtext, *Come with plenty of folding money, spend it fast, then get the hell out. Move here at your own, considerable, peril.* The situation has changed some in recent years, owing largely to rocky economic times up here, and so the message being sent by the present-day minions of state is of necessity more cordial. This is personally gratifying, since I love few things more than watching bureaucrats in a good grovel, even if they are sucking up to a bunch of Californians.

The other reason not to fish the river in the summer is the fish—the standard pellet-stuffed techno-trout excreted in impossible numbers from the modern American hatchery. In local angling circles, these trout arouse a species of contempt otherwise reserved exclusively for the Los Angeles Lakers. It's hard not to feel some sympathy for the fish. Anyone who's spent time watching them in the narrow concrete hatchery races understands that it gets ugly in there, an overcrowded, nose-scraping, fin-bitten world with absolutely no place to hide. The fish toughen up, but nothing they learn proves of the slightest use in the stream. In the end, they are temporary trout, doomed, fish out of water, until the first real cold snap croaks them. Pitiable it is, but few mourn their passing.

Even the river seems relieved to be rid of them. Having entertained thousands of visiting fishermen, and tens of thousands of visiting fish, the landscape grows a little ragged and strung out. Only autumn brings reprieve when, like a Moscow Circus bear after the closing performance, the Metolius climbs wearily down off the unicycle, sheds tutu and fez, and settles back into a life at least somewhat more congruent with its nature.

Though the shortening days and cooler weather foreshadow leaner times, the Metolius fares better in this regard than other rivers. It owes its existence to a large spring, where ancient underground seeps break to the surface in sufficient volume to produce a fair-size, fully functional trout stream from the very start. Such rivers are rare, and they never fail to impress. The flow remains cool and consistent, largely undisturbed by seasonal fluctuations, and the things that live here are sustained, more than anything else, by the simple unglamorous fact of predictability. From the trout's point of view, it is a climate-controlled world, and the biggest difference in going from summer to winter is that the food thins out a little and all the people leave.

Or almost all. A contingent of hard-cores hangs on past the summer season, fishing first the dwindling *Ephemerella* hatches and, later, the quirky hatch of *Dicosmoecus*, caddis the size of butterflies that shimmer like aspen leaves in the slant of October sun. Then small caddis again, and finally, when the bad weather blows in, a steady trickle of Blue-wing Olives that will last for months. And on a gray day in early December, sandwiched between the late-run salmon and the first few winter steelhead, this is where I've come for a day or two, to outfox the hedgehog.

At the moment, however, I don't feel terribly foxy. This morning I drove through a steady drizzle in the valley, a form of precipitation so routine in the sodden Northwest winters that it is inconsequentially called "dry rain." It occasions neither comment nor umbrella. Snow gusted through the passes, and here where I'd hoped to find sunshine, a tarnished-pewter sky reminds me that I haven't eluded the weather, just momentarily outrun it. Legs, a little wobbly from the two-hour drive, are shoved into overpants of forty-ounce wool, and on into waders. Two undershirts, a thick and venerable Pendleton, fly vest, rain jacket, fingerless gloves—a ritual that always reminds me of a priest gearing up to say Mass, though I find myself hoping, to greater overall effect.

Ponderosa needles accumulate in thick mats, cushiony and quiet, as I walk to a small bridge over this small river. Every trout stream has a starting point, though it is not necessarily where you start fishing. It's a place that you first stop for a look, both to check out the water and to check in, registering your arrival in some vaguely ceremonial way and giving your engagement a distinct beginning and so too a kind of shape. You watch, not so much for something in particular as for something in general, a kind of barometric reading that will communicate significances about the fishing to come. In the same intangible way that we know most of what we know about rivers, the water at the bridge transmits subtle meanings—nothing quite as specific as "information" (though this can certainly be gained), but more something felt or intuited. And on the basis of this something I'll choose a fly or a method or a place to fish that day—upstream to nymph the Cabin Pool, or a big caddis pattern in the pockets, or down to Wizard Falls to fish a tiny dry fly on glassy water. I don't always arrive at the best decision, sometimes not even a good one, but when I come to this bridge and study the water, I make a choice that I believe is not arbitrary, though I couldn't begin to articulate how or why. It may well be wishful delusion; it is most certainly all in my head. But I'm not alone in sensing these things.

What I always hope to see from the bridge, of course, are rising trout. But I don't figure to find them this morning, and the expectation is fulfilled in spades. Nothing but the smooth wash of current over a blue-gray bottom. In the loose taxonomies that fly fishermen use, the Metolius is a "nymphing river," a term that has nothing to do with the water and everything to do with the fish. Their response to dry flies, when no natural insects are on the water, is graphically unenthusiastic. A capable fisherman who prospects hard with floating flies will generally find a few takers, but for the most part blind-fishing like this doesn't pay out the kind of reward that's measured in fish. Day in and day out, nymphs will take most of the trout and all of the big ones.

So nymphs it is, and here the law has, with more than its customary unwittingness, effectively mandated a technique that is now almost universally practiced on the river. The Metolius has been designated as a "fly fishing only" river, which by legal definition in Oregon means that no additional weight may be attached to the leader, though weighted flies themselves are permitted. Much of the good nymphing occurs in deep, steadily paced runs with flies about as large and heavy as a good-sized grain of rice. Putting one of these on the nose of a trout in five feet of swift water is a problem. Without adding any weight to the leader, it becomes nearly impossible.

The solution that has evolved is not entirely palatable to all fly-fishing tastes. But foxes can't afford to be particular. To the business end of a long tippet, you attach a large (monstrous, if necessary, and it often is) weighted nymph. Two short sections of line are attached higher up the leader as droppers, and on these are tied smaller nymphs—the flies actually intended to attract the trout. Though the big nymph will occasionally take a fish, its prime requirement is sufficient heft to plummet the whole mess to the bottom. Hence a precise imitation is pretty much immaterial, though some approximation of a stonefly nymph is generally favored under the assumption that the fly can just as easily look like something as like nothing, and since stoneflies are the biggest bugs in the river, they'll do. Some of these patterns are phenomenally crude affairs, a pragmatic nod to their high rate of mortality on the rocky riverbed. The ideal ones are cheap and easy to tie, nondescript, and usually unchristened, since they're as temporary as a dimestore turtle and about as much in need of a name. Generically, they're known as "bullets," falling into that select category of flies designated not for what they represent but for how they behave.

From a fishing standpoint, the bullet-and-dropper setup casts with the grace of a turkey baster and hits the water like a roll of dimes. A #2 extra-long-shank hook wrapped in twenty-five turns of 5-amp fuse wire is heavier than a .30-.30 slug and correspondingly more lethal. This is the kind of projectile you want to keep close track of, so you lob it slowly and high overhead, with a deep deferential dip of the rod to prevent a collision with the big nymph, which could easily shatter a rod tip. Then, too, with multiple flies and droppers, the rig will collapse into a nightmare of monofilament coils and wind-knots at the first hint of hesitation or self-doubt in the caster. But when the whole affair is used skillfully, the fishing can be as extraordinary as the casting is vulgar.

It is curious to see how each fisherman will fix the limits of his own sport. Some use only the dry fly, others fish only to the rise, still others cast only feather-light rods or tiny patterns. No two anglers I've ever fished with defined their boundaries in quite the same way or devised quite the same rationale for what they did. We each map the borders of a world and fish in an envelope of our own making that is both intensely personal and flagrantly arbitrary. If pressed, we can give "reasons" for where we drew the lines, though often enough these are equally capricious and persuasive only to the likeminded. Our private strictures answer to a vision that encompasses a practical conduct, an aesthetic, and an ethic—which is to say, I suppose, that it is a philosophy. The multiple nymphs affixed to my leader are the kind of barbarism another fisherman might handle only with tongs. I string them up without a second thought.

The current below the bridge pinches at the throat of a pool, then fans evenly over alluvial rubble rich in food and resting places—the "classic" configuration, but rare on this river of bedrock bowls and fissured volcanic ledges. The trout will hold near the center, but I wade in at the tailout far below them for no other reason than that I have my own peculiarities and believe the thing must be done correctly. A pool exists as an entirety, a world within a world on the river, and it seems to me best approached with a consciousness of its nature. Begin far back, fish through the middle, and finish well beyond, recognizing in advance that some places will produce nothing, but the whole pool must be worked and its full measure taken with patience and attention if the thing is to be appreciated at all. The darkest water is usually best, and coming upon it gradually from the edges, shading from the visible to invisible, sanctions your anticipation. Only an understanding of shallows entitles you to depths. When you reach the water of greatest promise, you work a few intense, expectant inches at a time, and whether you raise something or not, you eventually move on. It has just the architecture of all experience, and there is as surely an ethic in the style of fishing as there is in living a life. Inside my envelope, there's no room for the prime-slicers, fishermen who cut a businesslike way to the best piece of water and help themselves to trout after trout. They fish in the calculation of cost/benefit ratios. Should these fall below projected levels, the fishing is no longer "worth it," and they let the matter drop as summarily as a hardscrabble farmer drowning a sack of kittens.

At the tailout, the cast of three nymphs hits the water—PLOOSH! Plip, plip—the ripples reverberating on the pool like a tiny sonic boom. The point fly is a big Simulator, all rooster hackle and peacock herl whose nearest relative is a bottle brush. First dropper is a Hare's Ear, the second a tiny Pheasant Tail. Swing, reach, lob. PLOOSH! Plip, plip. As long as the rhythm remains in steady threes, everything stays sorted out and working.

For the next hour-and-a-half, I fish slowly through the pool and catch a lone whitefish, the occupational hazard of Western fishing and the kind of small disappointment you can't take personally. They are, in any event, infinitely preferable to the marauding packs of chubs that roamed the trout streams of my youth. Now and then I change flies, tinkering first with the droppers then the point fly, each adjustment spiking the moment with hope. After you've fished for a while, the flies you use and the grounds for using them become entangled, and which one comes first no longer makes much difference. Sometimes, the reason is prior—a #16 tan caddis bounces down the riffle, and you knot on a #16 tan caddis. Sometimes, it's the fly—you tie on a big Royal Wulff and work backward to an explanation. That's about where I am today, trying first this, then that, all the time making up stories to rationalize my own choices. As much difference as this might make to me, it apparently makes none to the fish, which briskly continue not to bite.

Upstream, the small steel-and-concrete bridge weathered to dullness divides a gunmetal sky from its own reflection in the flat mirror of the pool. As in a neatly ruled perspective drawing, gray river and gray sky recede to a vanishing point hidden behind the bridge, which appears to span a vast chasm of air. The scene is a study in the undifferentiatedness that is the essence of a winter landscape. Most of the birds have sought lower altitudes and other animals their burrows. There are none of the sustaining particularities of other seasons. The streamside vegetation—waterhemlock, vetch, brookline, monkey flower, bog candle, corn lily, lupine—all have shriveled to an unvarying, husky brown, a reminder of the way that all dead things come to resemble one another. You are tempted to burden this with an emotional valence, to saddle it with the sadness of something lost; it takes effort to ignore what's missing and regard what's there.

Winter here is the land reduced to a lowest common denominator, condensed to innermost borders on the extremity of a year, with the river itself risen to the threshold of ice. The landscape curls inward to small sparks of life wrapped in bark or overlaid thickly with fat and fur, and shows to the world only a tough hide and dry brown spines.

I once read that all living things hinge on the most tenuous of astrophysical contingencies. Push the orbit of the earth just a little farther from the sun, just a few percent, and every molecule of water on the planet would freeze and all life vanish. Reduce the orbit by that same small amount, and the water would turn to vapor and the planet to an empty desert. The earth swims through space in the narrowest band of possibility circling round the sun, not all that different, really, from the trout stream at my feet, traveling its own ecliptic between lifeless banks.

The water is almost perfectly transparent, but in the deep runs and pools it takes on the tint of pale aqua, like a thickness of very old glass. Standing on the bridge, I can see fish six feet under the surface hugging the bottom. Mostly they're whitefish, with narrow wedged bodies and splayed pectoral fins. Pressed tight to the smooth bedrock bottom, they look like a dozen remora clinging to the belly of a shark. There are trout, of course, but these are fewer, and to my surprise I find a remnant of summer in two stocked trout, fin-bitten and strangely bluish. Not every hatchery fish comes out a genetic loser. The zygotic slushbuckets of the modern fish factory are not nearly so precise. Now and then, even a blind pig finds an acorn, and these two trout merely testify to the fact that when large numbers are involved, statistically tiny likelihoods will be represented. They may well survive. But I doubt it. The most exacting part of the season is yet to come.

Wild rainbows are down there too, liquid and shifting, as if coalesced from the current itself. Everything about them is a calculated un-obtrusiveness—their stream-colored backs, circumspect movement, their propensity to sidle somehow into invisibility. It takes good river eyes to see them through the wrinkled crosscurrents that cast fishlike shadows on the bottom. But if you wait, in time a billowy upwelling from beneath the bridge smooths the surface into perfect uniformity, as though a window pane were laid on the water. It drifts downstream and slowly dissipates, a momentary lens fixed on the secrets of the river. Before the window closes, I count four rainbows.

They hover over the bottom, where broken stone and ledgerock outcroppings shunt the current, and the friction of water against riverbed slackens its force. Life lived in this incessant streaming of atmosphere is almost impossible to imagine. Few things in a river are ever at rest, much as they may appear that way. There is always force and counterforce. A stall in the drift, the lee of a stone, any gap in the flow offers a trout sanctuary against the simple velocity of its world. So vital to existence are these modulations of current that the trout must perceive them in meticulous and complex detail. We're inclined to think of water as the fish's version of air, but I suspect a trout no more "feels" the current the way we feel a breeze than a bat "hears" its own sonic echo in the same way that we hear a shout or the ringing of a telephone. The reflected voice of a bat must inscribe an image in its brain that is essentially visual. It must hear solids and spaces. The lateral line on a fish detects vibration, perhaps conflating the senses of touch and hearing, to create an equally high-resolution picture. A fish feels its world, I imagine, in the way a bat hears—in three dimensions.

And what image must that world register? A running river is not the uniformity we see. Near the bottom is a chaos of eddies and whirlpools, backwashes and dead water and pillowy cushions. The flow is laminar with current layered on current, each a different configuration of effects, a different landscape for the fish—fierce hydraulic winds, jagged seams and breaks, shifting edges and dynamic, twisting columns. What we see as only water, the trout must sense as a vibrantly textured world. Current and obstruction sculpt the river into strata of force, fantastic canyons and rugged crags, deep washes and cliffs of turbulence, and the trout shapes its existence around them as closely and surely as an Anasazi.

Seeing these fish is deeply reassuring in a way that has little to do with fishing. It has been like this from my very first look at a trout stream twenty-five years ago in the limestone coulees of southwest Wisconsin. A few of us, brothers and friends, would scrounge up some transportation and head out, and for some years these spring creeks were the only trout waters I knew. Wild browns the color of clover honey hid among tangles of watercress and ranunculus, though their hold on the stream was weakened by thoughtless infusions of hatchery rainbows, unrestrained grazing, and neglect. On many of these tiny creeks, we never saw another fisherman. The trout were wary, skittish, and often beyond our abilities; each one landed was indescribably precious. We fished each stream with a weighty sense of proprietorship and the grave recognition that we might just be the only people on earth who cared that the trout were there at all, or who understood what they meant. The elation of opening day was always tempered with the fear that maybe this year, there would finally be no trout, that we would find something vital in the landscape had been extinguished and the world become a diminished place. Seeing the first trout of the year was more than a relief—it was a form of spiritual survival. The trout were still there; something important had continued.

Here in the West, trout streams are, comparatively speaking, a dime a dozen. I once worried that this abundance might make a difference, but it didn't. And if I should ever lose the reassurance that comes from just seeing trout, I'll quit fishing altogether. We all have our reasons.

In the winter of 1845, Thoreau walked from his cabin, down a snowy bank, and across the frozen face of Walden. Taking careful bearings from coves and spits of land on the shore, he began spudding holes through the ice and with line and lead sought to discover the deepest part his pond. On an east Cascade river, I plumb the pools with a trout fly that ticks unevenly across the streambed, telegraphing its contours and sounding its limits. That, I suppose, is why I've come, in the depth of a mountain winter—to rediscover what is continuous, irreducible, and rock bottom.

It comes, at first, in the form of two tiny gray wings. They appear quietly in the center of the pool and disappear with as little commotion. I overlook them at first. The wind has swirled in from the northwest, and overhead in the Ponderosas, dried pine needles shake loose and drift down, clustered in pairs like sprouting corn. They spear the surface of the water in quick dimples that at first I mistake for rises and soon come to ignore. When a few fish begin to feed amid the falling needles, I pay no attention. To miss the very thing you're looking for can be just this easy.

More gray wings begin to appear, floating up from the river and drifting downwind at eye level, impossible not to notice. I can tell at a glance they are Blue-wing Olives and, with a little luck, the beginning of something sublime. Quite unlike the Green Drakes and Golden Stone-flies—flashy, overscaled Disney-bugs that will hatch here in summer—the Blue-wing Olive is slight and unassuming, but deceptively tough, hardy, and reliable, a fox of a bug, undeterred, adaptable, a survivor. A Blue-collar Olive. Several years ago, and for various reasons, I found it prudent to set aside a certain category for those things that reach so deeply and so successfully into first principles that one's trust in them is absolute. Among them are Eureka Timberline tents, honeybees, Renzetti fly-tying vises, driftboats, Bridgeport Blue Heron ale, Swarovski optics, brown trout, Estwing rock hammers, the Grateful Dead, Stanley steel thermoses, and Blue-wing Olives.

Where the great number of aquatic insects that interest fly fishermen undergo but one emergence a year, the Blue-wing Olives just keep laying eggs and growing nymphs and hatching flies and feeding trout, heedless of calendars, even in winter. Strange as this may sound, they have always seemed to me to hatch best on the harshest days, though I'm willing to admit I might be imagining this or merely hoping it is so. Perhaps the incongruity of foul weather and emerging flies is stark enough to amplify a sense of the event through sheer contrast. Nevertheless, they hatch. And in the cold, rain, and spitting snow, they do it well enough, and so reward best those who endure the worst—one of the token moral symmetries at which the world, in rare moments, gives a grudging glimpse.

Then again, it's probably just an accident. But I do know that in warmer seasons, the sudden appearance of Blue-wing Olives has on countless occasions redeemed a slow day. On an icy December afternoon, they can save your soul.

In the time I take to clip off the nymphs, rebuild the leader to 6X, and tie on a small dry fly, a few more fish have begun to rise. Not many, perhaps seven or eight, and most of these are holding in a glassy slick well below the pool. I cut a wide circle away from the river to get below them and end up on the right bank, with the trout almost directly above me in sandy-bottomed, featureless water less than a foot deep. None are large. Across the river the bottom shelves off into deeper water and butts up against a volcanic ledge on the far bank.

The idea here is to reach out over the water with the rod, sidearm, and with a slightly overpowered cast, hook the fly and leader back in to the bank over the rising trout while laying the thick fly line toward the center of the stream, like a shepherd's crook lying obliquely on the current. This is the theory. The hitch is that I'm not terribly good at this sort of thing, especially when fish are rising. False-casting away from the trout, I measure out the distance anyway.

In our early twenties, my brother and I spent a summer of existential drift in a dingy northern Illinois town, haunting an even dingier little billiards parlor shooting nineball, another thing I'm not terribly good at. Passing up an easy play in the rotation, my brother leaned over and spent some time studying a fussy two-rail combination involving some potent left-English, for the win. Right idea for the right player, which we both knew he wasn't. A moment before stroking the shot, he simply looked up and explained, "You have to play like you know how." (He scratched. Two months later the owner of the place was shot dead at a snooker table, apparently miscalculating a drug transaction.)

Nevertheless, this seems to me an important idea regardless of the stakes, though what it generally ends up showing me is that I don't know how. The thirty-foot hook-cast to the first rise crashes miserably and spooks two fish. The next trout, farther out in the river, is more in line with my capacities, but eight or ten acceptable-looking drifts of the fly bring no response. I have just about persuaded myself that the fish is looking for emergers, when a Blue-wing Olive dun comes skating down the current, wings poised for the getaway, and disappears in a tiny vortex.

To Plan B: dressed on a #20 hook, its olive-brown body an eighth-of-an-inch long. Ten of them would fit in a thimble. Wings are a pair of watery-gray hen-hackle tips, the tail three glossy dun barbs of rooster hackle. Four horizontal turns of the same feather circle the base of the wings, spreading a radius of pontoons to float the fly. Fly tyers have their favorite children and this is mine—elegant, wispy, minimal. My fingers cannot produce a more faithful replica, and, resting on the water even ten feet away, I can't tell it from the genuine article. The fish are better at this, but then that's what they do for a living. Besides, in the end you please yourself in these matters.

To have begun with this fly, though, and tied it on at the outset would be going about it backward. Trout fishermen have their own ideas about which end of a thing to start at. They're apt to watch a trout or a piece of water, decide on a few flies suitable to the circumstance, loosely order the alternatives, and then work up the ladder rather than down, from the point of least promise to the greatest. The method is a little short on efficiency but offers something far more substantial—the concealed confidence of an ace in the hole, a way of converging on essences that lies beneath much of what fly fishermen do. This, I think, more than any consideration of technique accounts for the deep appeal of fishing upstream, always working to water as yet undisturbed and moving ever closer to the river's beginning. Every angler is an expert in the husbandry of hope, doling it out one spot, one cast, one fly at a time. But you must go gradually and play it close to your vest.

On the third drift the fly vanishes in a determined swirl, and the line cuts downstream in abrupt, boxerlike jabs, intensified by the current in the way that water seems always to magnify what's beneath it. I play the fish with a caution disproportionate to its size, gaining line when the trout stops, humoring it a little when it runs. The day is already looking lean, and bringing even a small fish to hand is a kind of validation, of its presence and your own. The way things are shaping up, I may not get another chance. The fish draws closer, and an instant before the hook pulls free I discover that it's a brown trout about a foot long, big-headed and snaky. He holds for a moment in the slack water beside me, unaware he's on his own again, then bolts to the channel.

Catching is not all of fishing, nor size the whole story in catching, but I regret losing the fish. The first trout I ever caught was a brown, and from that moment on they became for me the proto-species, the ur-trout to which all others aspired—a twice parochial attitude considering that the brown trout, of all salmonids in North America, is the only one that is not indigenous. Introduced from Britain in 1885, they were roundly condemned by American anglers as cannibalistic, ill-suited to the artificial fly, and ugly. That they displaced native fish cannot be disputed. Some of the fine, pristine brook trout streams of the East and Midwest are now occupied solely by browns, though as this century has amply shown, worse fates can befall a trout stream. Of their difficulty to catch there can be no doubt. On waters where such records are kept—the Madison River in Montana, for instance—perhaps one in ten trout caught is a brown, though browns and rainbows inhabit the river in near-ly equal numbers. I suspect the proportion of brown trout in the Metolius is smaller but have no reason to believe the catch ratio is any higher.

My almost-caught brown may be a descendant of fish stocked in decades past or perhaps its ancestors were put into Lake Billy Chinook, some forty miles downstream. The water flowing past my boots at this instant will, in half an hour, enter a narrow gorge. Half an hour later, it will emerge, flatten out briefly to accommodate a campground or two, flow beneath Bridge 99, and cut the next thirty miles through some for-midable country. For a while the river flows directly north, tight to the flank of Green Ridge on the east. A crude, rutted access road parallels the water on this bank. To the west the land ascends more gently in a broad apron to the foot of Mount Jefferson. Years ago, dismissed as unproduc-tive waste, the area was magnanimously deeded to the Warm Springs In-dians; from the Reservation, the river gets reinforcements—Candle Creek, Jefferson Creek, Sheep Creek, Code Creek, Camp and Racing Creeks, Rainy Creek, the Whitewater River. The broad plateau of the Metolius Bench finally turns the river southeast, where it enters Lake Billy Chinook.

In the first of these thirty miles, the drop of the river increases, and the current picks up speed and power. The pine forest thickens and the riverbanks grow a dense snarl of kinnikinnic, dog rose, serviceberry, hawthorn, snowberry, and alder, as punishing and impenetrable as concertina wire. The swift, deep water makes wading risky, and the few pools that have formed are clogged with jackstrawed timber and are effectively unfishable. And "Beyond this place," as ancient maps say, "there be dragons."

The river valley is hardly virgin wilderness, but it is a wonderfully wild place, worlds beyond the domestication of the upper river. Third-hand tales filter up of Green Drakes hatching in thousands and great wild rainbows that rise freely to them. But I rarely fish here. It's arduous, bushwhacking work, and my efforts have produced only a handful of whitefish and a few smaller trout. For all that, I still believe the stories. Conceived in the sense of promise that is always coupled with unspoiled places, these tales are assuredly true, even if there are no such flies and no such fish.

Eventually, the river and its stories drain into the lake. Oregon, I should point out, is "the Beaver State," an unwitting reference to the eagerness of its public officials and private utilities to throw up a dam at the first sniff of moving water. Wherever there is sufficient room for a bulldozer and a crate of dynamite, the Army Corps of Engineers trips gaily in to do what it does best. Round Butte Dam undoubtedly proved a triple delight, a concrete-and-steel stopper across the Deschutes River, directly below its confluence with the Metolius and Crooked rivers, submerging what must have been, once, one of the prettiest spots in the desert. The resulting backup, Lake Billy Chinook, was subsequently hosed full of water-skiers and fish.

Thirty minutes after the first Blue-wing Olives appear, the hatch begins to dwindle and the rises cease. It happens like this sometimes. The winter cracks open just long enough and wide enough to show what's inside, and then clamps shut. The last few flies slip downriver quietly, oblivious to the hazards of a minute before.

Night will fall quickly on the short winter day, and the slushy roads through the passes will soon begin to freeze. Still, I'm reluctant to head home. There's time to try one last place upstream, and I drive the short distance to Camp Sherman—until recently a collection of structures with just enough density to hit cartographic critical mass. It appeared as a speck on the map, but was a town only by an act of imagination. A bridge crossed the river there, and a dozen summer homes strayed up and down the banks. There were rental cabins and a general store, one end of which doubled as a post office. At some point, though, the place contracted a case of galloping development, with RV Parks, A-frame subdivisions, and pre-fab log houses—an infestation almost universally, and with some justification, laid at the feet of the Californians. What was once a land-scape is being slowly and irretrievably nibbled to lots.

Yet a certain provisional harmony still exists between the human habitations and the river that winds among them, which I suppose is the least one might expect from a few hundred people who've sought their happiness on the banks of a trout stream. In some regards, the town re-calls the bucolic English hamlets I've seen that had trout waters running through them—Bibury on the Coln, or Ashford-in-the-Water on the banks of the Wye. But so far the citizens of Camp Sherman have resisted the English obsession for building weirs in the river, dredging the chan-nels, and erecting quaint stone walls on its banks—less the consequences of utility or aesthetics, I think, than a certain brand of fear. Much of British history has been propelled by a theological mistrust of wildness, and coming to the New World they brought their apprehensions with them, carefully salted away among the hogsheads of bully beef, ship's bis-cuit, and Bibles that ground to a stop on Massachusetts granite. But once here, fear gained a less-certain foothold, was pursued less fanatically, or perhaps just thinned out in the overwhelming solvent of the continent. It never vanished altogether, just changed, and the American appetite is less for moral conquest than commerce—not exactly the ethical high ground, I realize, but it has had the inadvertent effect of leaving those things and places of little marketable value at least somewhat untouched.

Camp Sherman, though being transformed from "town" to "going concern," nonetheless retains a certain picturesqueness, and the water upstream remains, to my eyes, the loveliest on the river. The more leisurely gradient of the terrain slows the current. It is more obviously a spring creek here. The banks are lower, the water more placid, and even at this time of year aquatic plants flourish in scattered patches of green. The whole effect of the place is utterly calming. Here and there the strange tubers of waterhemlock float in slow eddies, broken from the streamside plants and sent to colonize other banks. They have the strange manlike shape of mandrake root or ginseng.

There's a great satisfaction in studying a trout stream, reading its water, and by your own foxiness discovering the secrets of its fish. But sometimes, serendipitous discoveries please the most. Finally, there are places in a river that must simply be stumbled upon. Their logic, if it is ever understood at all, comes only after the fact. Refusing to advertise themselves, they remain hidden and so remain yours, at least as far as you can tell, which is far enough.

The spot I've come to fish is of just this kind, a small trough on the far bank so unobtrusive that there's no need for the overhanging branches that conceal it. This small spot has two claims to virtue. Even in summer there are no hatchery fish here, and almost invariably, it will give up a trout to a dry fly. Even when no insects are hatching. Even in winter.

I make the first casts to the tail end, less in the anticipation of raising a fish than in raising the pleasure of anticipation. One cast to the dark water and the fly vanishes. Moments later a wild rainbow splashes in the river at my feet. It is olive-gold, almost brassy on the flanks, and down the side runs a ruby stripe as vivid and extravagant as a wild strawberry.

Lhude sing Goddamm.

4

The Thing
with Feathers

"Hope" is the thing with feathers—

That perches in the soul—

—Emily Dickinson

As far as I've been able to determine, Emily Dickinson didn't know a fly rod from a fly swatter, so I'm at a loss to explain how she so completely understood trout flies.

I find it impossible to speak about fishing at all without using the word "hope," because angling fits into a category of human experience that is rooted more in expectation and possibility than in some kind of achievement or fulfillment. Things like courtship, artistic creation, religion, and fly fishing (which is more than incidentally related to each of these) seem to me of a piece. All of them presume goals, of course—marriage, artifact, salvation, and trout—which certainly shape the enterprise, but they don't necessarily define its meaning or the source of its enjoyment. Quite the contrary—the significance of the whole experience, and much of our pleasure in participating in it, stems precisely from the prospect of not attaining the object. Lovers, poets, religious madmen, and anglers seem to me to have this in common—they live for the impassioned anticipation of an uncertain thing.

All of this may seem little more than mere rationalization for the fact that we spend more time fishing than we do catching fish, and so may as well make the best of it. There's some truth to this: few of us would fish if the object were perpetually unachievable, if fish were caught only rarely and then with extreme difficulty. If anticipation were largely vain, it couldn't sustain us. But it is equally true, I think, that few of us would fish if trout were caught on every cast. Reduce anticipation to certainty, and there's little left to appreciate. Catching fish is undeniably a pleasure, and I'd rather do it than not, but there is a pleasure too in fishing, the savor of pure possibility always on the brink of realizing itself—or not—and the attraction of fishing has much to do with the keenness of expectation and desire urged against the uncertain and unpredictable.

That is, it has much to do with the peculiar pleasure of hope, which balances on the slightest of perches between unfulfillable wishfulness and foregone conclusion, and looks precisely like a trout fly. Spun with dubbing, wrapped in hackle, and whipped in the thread, the hope at the heart of angling is fashioned from the thing with feathers, and if a trout fly seems pretty flimsy to be bearing this kind of weight, I dare say that most of us have at times pinned our hope on a good deal less.

Fly fishing begins with the fly, a fact often obscured in the seductive technomadness of modern tackle, where each new rod or line or gadget is unveiled to messianic trumpets, the redeemer of your miserable angling equipage. But the fly is always prior. In the whole lumbering, clanking warehouse of an onstream angler, the fly is the starting point, the single piece of gear we carry from which the entire sport can be reconstructed. If the principal problem is to catch a trout, the solution begins in selecting or tying a fly with the greatest likelihood of appealing to any individual fish. From there, you must devise a way to cast it, since the insubstantiality of the fly makes it incompatible with ordinary tackle.

Hence a relatively long, limber rod and a line with sufficient mass to flex it, given the absence of any weight in the fly. The need to distance the fish, hence the fly, from the thick line gives rise to the leader. A convenient place to store the line in readiness suggests a reel. A box to hold the flies, a vest to hold the box, waders to hold the fisherman, and an assortment of gizmos and aids to minister to all sorts of needs and procedures, and so on in a branching regression that eventually encompasses all the stuff we carry and the way we use it.

Moreover, beginning with the fly, you can not only generate a single, modern, fully equipped fly fisher, but the entire history of fly angling. Perhaps nothing argues more for the primacy of the fly itself than the fact that they have changed so little over so many centuries. This is true not only of basic appearance and design, but of specific patterns and combinations of materials that date back to some of the earliest written records, and who knows how far beyond them. The fly is the historical constant, and the entire evolution of fly-fishing equipment, techniques, and practices has been only a series of changes to improve the ways we manage this unchanging fact.

But the fly is an end as well as a beginning. It forms the terminus of all our preparations, study, practice, and observation. Once it is freely drifting on the current, the matter is pretty much out of our hands. We've done all we can to make the fly and its behavior convincing, and now consolidate desire, anticipation, and hope into this bit of floating fluff. The rest is up to the trout.

The angler's part of fly fishing begins and ends with the fly, and everything in between—the tackle, the planning, the preparations, the trip, the reading and wading of water, the casting—all are ancillary, mere vehicles for delivering the fly from vise to trout, for transferring it from one set of jaws to another.

The ironies are delightful. The grossest and most substantial of our equipment exists solely to serve the slightest; a thousand dollars' worth of gear is given meaning by a quarter's worth of chicken feather and wire. Moreover, all of it, the meticulousness at the vise, the careful knots, the selection and balance of gear, the arrangements and precautions, the discipline to master the cast, the science and system, the study of water—all is focused on the ultimately crude reenactment of an event that happens a million times a minute in the natural world. Nature is the most exacting of models, and in fly fishing nothing hints more emphatically that we are on the right track than the difficulty of our labors.

These ironies and their grand disproportion give fly fishing a distinct form. Grosser things serving finer ones, the clumsy and tangled labor for the ordinary, the consequential hinging on the apparently slight —these imbue the whole affair of fly fishing with a dramatic structure, like a novel. Emma's insult on Box Hill or Huck Finn's resolution to go to hell are but literary versions of a drifting fly. All are local and specific points at which something is on the verge of unfolding. In its details and techniques, fly fishing may be poetry, but the fact of the fly gives it the shape of narrative.

As both commencement and terminus, as the point of departure and culmination, the trout fly is the nexus of the sport, a tiny point from which radiate a thousand strands of our engagement. Despite its reliance on the line, fly fishing is not linear. It is radial and weblike. At the center is a rising trout, and millimeters above its nose is the fly. From it, paths trace outward to the engineering and art of tackle making, to geology and hydrology, botany and birds, aquatic and terrestrial insects, landscapes, books, history, photography, and a thousand other intersecting filaments that lead just as far as you wish to go.

No one, to my mind, has appreciated or articulated this sense of connections better than Darrel Martin, and it is scarcely an accident that he is a fly tyer. His unassumingly titled book, *Fly-Tying Methods*, is no ordinary treatment of the subject. It ranges broadly through a complex of relations that begins at the vise and ends up as one man's contextualization of the trout fly, a task that at various points dwells on aquatic plants and their significance, Aristotle, photomicrographic details of the structure of fly-tying materials, the drawing pencils best used to shade a mayfly wing and the pen nibs to produce a particular kind of stippling, the mechanics of hook stress, the architecture of a single feather, the anatomization of insects, theories of classicism and romanticism, painting, and philosophy, among other things. His efforts raise into three dimensions what is typically rendered in two, and it is from such meditations, as eclectic, ordered, or random as the individual temperament, that trout flies are born.

I find it significant that of the gear we use, the fly is the only item that must necessarily be made by hand. Granted, some are tied on machines. There are the large-volume overseas tying operations, with row upon row of women and girls seated at electrically powered, sewing-machinelike rotary vises, that call to mind photographs of 1920s garment workers. Even so, the flies aren't tied *by* the machines, and the handcrafted product will always carry with it something of the craftsman, even if it is only a simple interpretation of how the thing should be done.

A trout fly is impressed with the personality of the fly dresser, and this is most obviously the case with the kind of professional tyers who don't traffic in large quantities of flies, but in ideas—designing new patterns, devising new techniques, appropriating new materials, and revising, sometimes reinventing, the craft. And it is also true of ordinary anglers who tie their own flies for their own fishing primarily because the experience of particular times and places have imbued them with very specific ideas about how fly design ought to be approached, about what makes a good fly, about materials, about how trout behave.

Professionals or amateurs, they cannot help but stamp their efforts with something of themselves. This is certainly most evident in the patterns we privately develop or the innovations we contrive (and it is a rare tyer who does not have many of these), but the personality of the tyer expresses itself in conventional and standard dressings as well. Ask a hundred fishermen to tie the perfect Adams, and no two of the flies will look precisely alike. The tilt of the wing, the wrap and density of the hackle, the angle of the tail, the thickness and taper of the body—all answer to something slightly different in each tyer's imagination.

In short, a fly tyer labors less to replicate an artifact or execute a set of instructions than to approximate an idea—to approximate, in fact, an ideal. At the heart of the fly tyer, I think, is a Platonic conception, or rather, a set of them—the perfect Blue-wing Olive dun, the perfect March Brown nymph, the perfect emerging caddis. The perfect fly forms the unspoken presupposition, the thing "that perches in the soul" of fly tying. We don't simply wish to make a "better fly"; we do it by aspiring *to* something that exists only as an idea. The Platonic fly is a benign Moby-Dick, a tantalizing phantom briefly glimpsed as it swims through the mind—some design, some material, some combination of materials, some precise shade of color that waits to be found and will, if only in some local circumstance, prove the answer. Questioned point blank about this notion of ideals, a fly tyer will undoubtedly deny it: There can be no such thing as the perfect fly. But then they are answering not as tyers but as fishermen, whose job it must always be to measure just how far effort falls short of intention.

But the Platonic conception, the belief that the perfect fly exists as an idea yet to be discovered, is the engine that drives the craft and the craftsman, and hope is the fuel.

Based upon our understanding of trout, our observations of the natural world, our experiences as fishermen, and our aesthetic inclinations, these ideas vary widely, as do the avenues of approaching them. Consider for example the fly designs of Gary LaFontaine, whose style issues from the methods of science. Born from underwater observation, his flies are abstracted to the essentials of reflected and refracted light, and strive less to mimic an insect than to reproduce physical properties. The ideal is approached through closely reasoned generalizations based upon specific instances. At the other end of the spectrum, at least in my view of it, are flies from tyers like Jack Gartside, whose designs, tying style, and selection of materials seem improvisational, almost spontaneous, the product of a man who has fishlike instincts and whose ideal is grounded less in bugs than in a notion of bugginess. Still again, there's Dick Talleur, whose flies embody an exacting craftsmanship, a vision of materials precisely arranged. His perfect fly reaches first to an idea of form. There are yet other tyers who seek to replicate in exact detail the tails, body segments, wings, and legs of an insect and produce an artificial that is indistinguishable from life. And these seem to me little more than stunts, pure disembodied technique that looks no further than mere duplication as its highest achievement. I doubt such flies catch fish—doubt that they are intended to—which is probably the most damning thing that can be said about them. They are literally without hope.

But the serious tyer, whether skilled or not, prolific or occasional, is propelled by an idea, and I've never met one who wasn't at some point seized by a glimmer of something that might move him closer to the Platonic pattern. He gathers or seeks out materials and immediately sits down to the vise to incarnate his idea. Darrel Martin points out, and shrewdly I think, that "Fly tying is a form of fishing," and this is what a fly tyer fishes for: a kind of knowledge, about trout and the natural world, that comes from persistent attempts to realize the perfect fly. Michelangelo and modern medical students alike have sketched the details of the human body. We imitate to understand, and the perfect imitation, the Platonic trout fly, is an emblem of perfect understanding.

Beneath it is the presupposition that all trout, or even a single trout at different times, rely on consistent mechanisms for distinguishing fraudulent food from the real thing. This may or may not be true, but without the assumption, fly tying is directionless, and the rationales for its styles disintegrate. Like philosophy and religion, fly tying is fundamentally naive; its first principles are always matters of faith. And this may explain why so many tyers are opinionated and iconoclastic—holders of the true creed—and at the same time open-minded, eclectic, foxy, always with an eye toward the half-truths of others for a hint of how to further their own.

To make a thing by hand and in so doing give it the imprint of yourself is a distinctly godlike activity. You sit down, deity of the vise, and from bags of feather and fur, people the world of your fly boxes with creations made in your own image, that answer only to the design or delusion of your own mind. That the final products turn out as equivocally as the creations of other gods at other times merely reinforces the connection.

I am a teacher by vocation, a fisherman by avocation, and if there is any connection between the two, it is here. Both teaching and fly tying begin with things half-formed, with bare hooks and brains, waiting for the impress of purpose. And while tempered wire and chicken fluff are infinitely more tractable stuff than the mind of a twenty-year-old, with both, the nature of the material must be respected. But teaching and tying, finally, are profoundly egocentric crafts, and both are ultimately autobiography.

By most standards, I don't tie all that many flies—perhaps seventy or eighty dozen a year, though probably a bit fewer these days—and the ma-

jority are standard patterns. But it's a pretty good bet that I could identi-
fy one of my flies in a lineup, not because they are exceptionally good
(they aren't) or because they are unusually shabby (I hope they aren't),
but simply because, in small ways, they look different. They consolidate
and embody particular ideas that I have about fly dressing, only a few of
which have anything directly to do with trout. Most are personal interpretations of tradition—about perpendicularity of hackle on a dry fly, the
tightness or looseness of dubbing on any given pattern, the reach of a
wing case on a nymph—that have really little other function than to be
part of a "well-tied fly" as that term is understood by tyers. In short, they
are largely aesthetic elements rather than practical ones, part of the con-
ventions and forms that govern fly tying, and for that reason are often arbitrary.

Pursuing this line of thinking, I have more than once found myself
drawn into argument about the nature of fly tying—is it a craft or, as so
commonly called, an art? To me there can be no doubt—it is quite clearly a craft. True, it has an aesthetic, but then so does motocross racing. And
fly tyers are "artistic" in the way we use the term to acknowledge polished
technical skill. But so is the guy who builds a scale model of the Eiffel
Tower out of twist-ties, or the bow-tied enigma I used to watch on the old
Ed Sullivan show, who kept twenty china plates spinning atop wobbling
wooden rods, lunging back and forth between them to the cadence of
some frantic tune, twirling them anew before they crashed to the stage.
Hardly art, though I concede that today his performance might be looked
upon as a metaphor for something or other and earn him an NEA grant.

These debates over art or craft lead in one of two directions, de-
pending on who's involved. Sometimes, they leap quickly away from fly
tying into the nature of art, from there to philosophy, and then invariably
to the gloomy vapors of poststructuralist critical theory, upon which I in-
voluntarily but gratefully fall into a deep, narcotic slumber. Other times,
I'm pinned into a corner and forced to admit the truth: that I don't much
really care for the kind of framed and signed exhibition-grade full-dress
salmon flies that hang by the dozen on dentist-office walls these days. I
am awed by the technical virtuosity and fantastic skill of the fly dresser.
I've tried to tie them, and they are insanely difficult to do well. But as art,

I'm forced to admit, they leave me cold, at which point I am roundly pronounced an idiot. When compromise is possible, fly tying is relegated by mutual agreement to that vague and recently created category, "folk art," and the matter rests there.

I think the desire to regard fly tying as an art stems in part from a kind of self-aggrandizement—less because we so highly value art than because the idea of "craft" has become so devalued in our age, appropriated by the glitter-and-glue Christmas-card crowd and those who fashion grisly knickknacks of sequined felt and yarn for the enhanced storage of paper clips. Against this background, the "art" of fly tying is perhaps a bit more understandable.

As a craft, fly tying is really the most conspicuous example of the general propensity among fly fishermen to build their involvement in the sport from the ground up. They tinker incessantly, making tackle or modifying it, inventing and experimenting, tailoring and improving to increase the usefulness, pleasure, or beauty of the things they use. Fly fishing contains a strong vein of do-it-yourselfism that allows each angler to fashion his own most satisfying version of the sport.

Having confessed already to one heresy, about full-dress salmon flies, I may as well burn myself at the stake and admit that I would rather chew little balls of tin foil than reread Izaak Walton's *Compleat Angler*, a book universally admired among fly fishermen, almost none of whom have read it. The singing milkmaids numb me. Walton's much-vaunted literary virtues seldom rise above "quaintness," which is to say, not very far. But the book offers one redeeming fragment, a section in which Walton, all his disingenuous pomposity aside, eagerly details a somewhat involved method of breeding maggots for bait. It is the one part of the book that convinced me the man actually fished, partly because raising and tending bait is not really all that far from fly tying, and partly because a loving enthusiasm for something like maggots illustrates the extent to which fishermen have always valued a sense of wholeness and self-containedness about what they do. Old angling books in general are filled with this kind of wonderfully arcane "how-to" information—about cutting and working wood for rods; weaving horsehair lines and dressing them with concoctions of sheep tallow, beeswax, and linseed oil; about drawing gut and waterproofing boots.

It goes without saying, of course, that such information was far more crucial then than it is now. In centuries past, commercially manufactured tackle was comparatively scarce, a commodity for the man of means, and it was an accepted part of angling life that most of what you had, you made. Yet the words of old angling authors reach beyond simple utility. You can hear in them delight, passion, pride, and conviction. There were not simply things to do or make, but things to be done or made well. One author explains precisely the breed, age, condition, and color of horse whose tail makes the strongest fishing line; how to select the hairs; the best time of year and method for collecting them. Another is concerned with the minutiae of carrion—the best type of meat and process of treating it that will produce the most succulent blowfly maggots. From the voice of such instructions and their absorption in detail, it is clear that such matters transcended the mere necessity of having line or bait. They were deeply engaging parts of fishing itself.

I see little reason to lament the past, however. If these old skills and the need for them have become obsolete, the underlying impulse persists. Just incidentally, I think that the fear of losing this impulse for wholeness in the sport underlies much of the alarm prompted by what has been perceived as the "Yuppie invasion" of fly fishing. I suspect that all the concern really stems from an invasion of pure technology rather than people. On Friday, a Boston neurosurgeon is standing stark naked in a fly shop wielding a fistful of major credit cards. On Saturday, he's fully outfitted in the front of a driftboat being rowed down the Green or Bighorn, catching the biggest trout he may ever see in his life. It isn't some gunnysack mentality that's worrisome. This guy probably enjoys the experience of being outdoors and appreciates the beauty of rivers as much as anyone. Tackle dealers and guides love him. But to the long-time fisherman, inveterate tinker, catcher of bugs, and tyer of flies, there is a hole in the middle of the neurosurgeon's sport that threatens to transform fly fishing. The approach seems antiseptic, too few hands laid on too few things to satisfy a fisherman's desire for wholeness.

Many anglers view this with deep mistrust, though I think their apprehensions are groundless. The sense, gained through an idea of "craft," that what a fisherman does is somehow all of a piece remains the most solid, and solidly felt, kind of tradition, one of fly fishing's most enduring and robust continuities. It is perpetuated by the staggering number of people who are crafting cane rods these days, and by an equal number hand-machining fine reels. If we can't quite do these things ourselves, we nonetheless perpetuate the impulse by winding and finishing our own rods, collecting and observing insects, taking photographs, fussing with gear and fine-tuning tackle, by studying maps and political agendas, and by a host of things at some remove from the trout itself.

Most of all, we perpetuate it in fly tying, which provides a connectedness both through its craft and through its materials. Perhaps because so many of these materials began as living things, they invest fly tying with a kind of authenticity and rootedness, like a potter's clay or weaver's wool. There are, of course, synthetic materials, and like most tyers, I will use them—though only when I believe they will make a more effective fly. I never tie with them, as I do some natural ones, simply because they are beautiful to look at or pleasing to work. A fly that takes shape from feathers, furs, and hairs may be an imitation, but it is not faked or ingenuine. That a trout believes a trout fly to be something alive comes as no surprise to a tyer. There's life in the materials, and that we catch trout on feathers and fur, lure one animal with another, strikes me as a perfectly proportioned and symmetrical idea, and also an ancient one.

Few craftsmen have at their disposal the fly tyer's number and variety of materials. As I write this from my study, I sit looking at my tying "bench"—a crude structure of varnished pine one-by-twelves arranged into shelves and compartments that house dozens of boxes and hundreds of small bags of material, as well as books, tools, and things hung on hooks. It stands over six feet high and at nearly seven feet long is the largest piece of furniture I own. And everything in it (as well as everything in two adjacent cabinets of drawers) is for fly tying. Next to the bench is a traveling kit, bulging with 2,000 hooks, a full set of tools, and several hundred bits of this and that. I consider myself only moderately equipped. But visually, it is arresting—a little like the displays in a fly shop, where the eye dwells on immense diversities of color, subtleties of mottle and vermiculation, palettes of texture, and I find my materials thoroughly satisfying even when I'm not tying with them.

They are, though, equally pleasing to the hand. No material is simply tied. It is learned, its quirks and behaviors slowly identified, its virtues and foibles gradually understood. Some behave well and tie easily, and these are the first favorites. Others have minds of their own, and over time you learn ways to compensate for them, outwit them, coax them into order. And as you come to know materials, a few take on almost mystical qualities, for their beauty and handling and, not least, their attractiveness to fish.

For me, no fly tied with hare's ear dubbing can disappoint. Pheasant tail, peacock herl, and deer hair invest a pattern with the highest promise. It's possible, even likely, that I first caught fish on flies fashioned of these materials. So I tied them often and fished them better and took more fish, which increased my confidence and prompted me to use them frequently, and so on in the thoroughly ordinary type of cycle where causes and effects slip in and out of one another. But what remains of it all is a belief that something remarkable inheres in the materials themselves, and my faith in them is deep and automatic.

Of the mystical materials, none is more potent than grizzly hackle, or any of the "variant" hackles that are barred, flecked, or figured with the alternating patterns of life. Partly, I like them because of my obsession within an obsession. Like many, I am a hackle junkie, a compensatory fetish born in the deprivations of youth. I came of fly-tying age in a time when fine hackle was virtually unavailable to the average tyer, and read with agonized envy of those who knew Andy Miner or Harry Darbee and were the beneficiaries of some of those legendary feathers. When prime genetic hackle necks became available, I couldn't have enough of them—still can't—and I love them like children.

Foremost among them is an irreproachable #1 ginger-grizzly saddle-patch given to me by hacklemeister Henry Hoffman. Its long, narrow feathers, tightly banded in honey and cream, droop like tendrils, lush as an orchid. It deserves its own bodyguard—to protect it from me if no one else. At first resolved never to touch it, I gradually became torn between its immaculate intactness and the possibilities it represented. One day, seized by an idea of the perfect fly, I thieved a single feather from which I tied nine delicate *dorotheas*, and that, as they say, was the beginning of the end. Bagged and pegged, it hangs now, snatched half-bald in the service of hope.

A fly tyer's materials are the anticipation of an anticipation. I wouldn't go so far as say to that the passion and energy with which we craft the thing with feathers somehow hints darkly at the dearth of hope in other regards. But there does seem to me this much truth in it: Tying a fly and fishing it scales the matter down to manageable size. Catching fish is, often enough, simply not that difficult, and to hang your hope on it is to make the universe play by your rules for a little while. This, I think, is the unconscious genius of the fisherman and the brilliance of fishing.

5

Feed That Jones

Man's chief difference from the brutes lies in the
exuberant excess of his subjective propensities. . . .
Prune his extravagance, sober him, and you undo him.
—*William James,* The Will to Believe

Anything that can get drunk, he reasoned, must have
some soul. Perhaps this is all "soul" really means.
—*Thomas Pynchon,* V.

To see any species at its most ridiculous, you must observe it in the procreative act. We are never so absurd as when we cannot help ourselves. If anything, this is truer still of fishing. At least sex, under ordinary circumstances, demands a pause every now and then and has prudently built in the nuisance of requiring at least two people. But fishing can go on indefinitely for hours, day after week after month, and you need involve only yourself. Technically speaking, it doesn't even require the fish. But if you're destined to fish, you accept the inevitable that in stoking your habit you will, in the end, do just about anything and so from time to time are bound to appear peculiar, even in your own eyes. A well-chosen passion has a certain redemptive power—it can save you from many things. "Yourself," however, is not one of them.

And why should it be? There is nothing interesting about a resistible urge.

In the twelfth century Saint Hildegarde of Bingen, German nun and mystic, had a divine vision in which she was commanded to eat fennel every day—an exceptionally bizarre injunction, to be sure, though still far from the benchmark set by the heavenly directive that separated the Chosen People from their foreskins. So Hildegarde ate her fennel religiously and right up to the end. History is less clear about whether she enjoyed it, but I'm nonetheless compelled by the cultivation of any private weirdness that seems to issue from sources beyond our control. And if you're driven to anything, to fennel or fishing, sometimes it's best to put aside questions about who's doing the driving and just take in the view instead, if for no other reason than to find your way back. You can run through some pretty strange territory.

Like most serious fishermen, I have practically made a second career out of chasing wild geese. There are always the rumors, the hints overheard in whispered fly-shop conversations that cease abruptly when you come closer; the tantalizing blue wiggle on a $7^1/_2$-minute quadrangle; the little high-country pond that no one seems to know anything about—a trout fisherman's irrefutable proof that it's brimming with fish. Sometimes the lure is big trout, growing bigger even as you think about them, in miles of foaming and unwadable river bound by sheer rock walls. Sometimes it's numbers, a remote creek where pan-sized trout lie exactly where they ought to in textbook perfection and play by the rules. Or the best score of all, the goose I have chased the longest, with the deepest obsession and the least success—the modest little stream, undiscovered by the others, pristine and trout-filled and not down on any map because, says Melville, "True places never are."

Whatever it might be, no clue is too improbable to follow up. No scuttlebutt seems too outrageous, no suspicion too farfetched. Every rabbit is dogged to its hole, and each time you take a chance, though not a risk, since "failure" is a concept without meaning in this kind of thing.

To find wild geese, you must seek them where they live, which is almost always a place called "the middle of nowhere," whose only known approach is the highway of excess. There are the caffeinated all-night drives; the subsequent stumble-footed fishing in a vaguely hallucinogenic buzz of sleep-deprivation and endocrine imbalance. The days subsisting on beer nuts, Twinkies, and infrared hot dogs turning forlornly on oiled bogeys, and all purchased from a crossroads service station whose peeling sign advertises with inadvertent candor, "Food/Gas." There are frantic, marathon fly-tying sessions, since what you'll need at points unknown is, well, unknown. And of course, the maps. A dozen tight-scale topographicals are seined and studied, courses plotted, streams marked, backup plans and lists of gear scribbled on the back. In the tired euphoria of 3 A.M., someone speaks up, obliged, he says, to point out that the whole plan doesn't stand a chance, and we'll be lucky to take one fish between us. We all nod gravely and hastily agree that, yes, it'll no doubt turn out like all the other trips. But this is part of the thing, too, and we act like adults for a few minutes, a mandatory concession to the fact that all of us have reached the far side of thirty. Then we plunge back to the maps, and from wide-eyed departure to red-eyed return, the whole thing is fueled by uncut adrenalin and the barely concealed certainty that this time it will all pan out.

So we go with the plan or junk it, find what we're looking for or don't, catch fish or not. The details are as insignificant as they are mutable. At the heart of the thing, we've traveled somewhere new or different, logged some river time, fished ourselves stupid, and spiked a fix that will keep us high for many days—weeks if someone happens to bring a camera.

This will hardly seem like eccentric behavior to anyone who fishes much, and in fact, it's pretty tame fare measured against the handful of genuinely clinical types I know who draw no lines between a fishing trip and an extended psychotic episode. Their houses are merely mailing addresses. They live on the road, sleeping if they sleep at all on car seats or on the ground, usually in their clothes but sometimes in waders if the fishing is good. To save daylight for fishing, they drive only after dark and tie flies en route. They talk incessantly of fishing, even while they're doing it, which is almost all the time, and subsist, I'm certain, on tiny pellets of enriched plutonium since the occasional meal of beer and bologna could scarcely power these ballistic frenzies.

Still, I suppose the last refuge of the lunatic is to insist that the world is home to greater fools than himself, and in the end my complicity is a matter of record.

Or rather, was. In the last few years, circumstances have scaled back this kind of thing, and not altogether unmercifully. Serious binge-fishing is the romantic side of the sport—obsession played out as quest—and like many forms of romance, it is by and large a young man's game. From time to time, friends still phone when they're mounting one of their prolonged insanities, but I usually decline, and they contend, unfairly, that I no longer have the stomach for it. The liver would be a better guess. Nonetheless, thirty-five years ago, I toddled off to Turtle Creek with a cane pole and worms and returned with a six-inch smallmouth and a monkey on my back. I ate the bass and have been feeding the monkey ever since. Fortunately, it isn't particular. These days, when I cannot go elsewhere, I go otherwise. If the trout fishing is too distant or the time too short or the season closed, I fish for something else.

This isn't quite the simple solution it appears. Every angler harrows the underwater underworld, dividing the fish of promise from the fish of perdition, the worthy from the damned. The process is curiously arbitrary, based more on custom, tradition, and local circumstance than on any particular merits that a species possesses or is perceived to possess. Certain crude distinctions even acquire an institutional validation by the state, as Fish and Game departments chart a somber line between "game fish" on the one hand, and "coarse fish," "rough fish," or, as the category has almost universally become known, "trash fish," on the other.

From here, anglers pattern their own idiosyncratic hierarchies and byzantine rationalizations, compared to which the hairsplitting theology of Aquinas is but brain surgery with a butter knife. You are a bass fisherman, or rather, a smallmouth or largemouth angler, or a walleye fisherman, or crappie fisherman, or a catfisherman, or Atlantic salmon angler, and the contention among them, like most disputes in life, grows vehement in direct proportion to the inconsequentiality of the stakes. We defend our imaginary fiefdoms with the tiny ferocity of hummingbirds. It may merely typify the modern age's spectacular infatuation with specialization, where endless miles of mallspace are devoted to shops selling only Swedish dental floss or designer shoestrings or wax lips, where cars are not washed but "detailed," where the halls of academentia are papered over with treatises on "The Images of Ceramic Pots in the Late Novels of Henry James," or "Pickles of Enlightenment: the Significance of the Cucumber in Anglo-French Relations (1760-1761)."

Then again, the stakes may be weightier than they appear, for the esteem that fishermen bestow on the chosen quarry is reflexively conferred on ourselves. No matter that it's circular and self-validating, that the particular magnificence of, say, the muskie fisherman is appreciated mostly by other muskie fishermen. That is enough, and may well explain the passion with which we defend our choices. In an authentic bit of human folly, we gather up our own social categories—the slime dwellers, the blue collars, the wannabes, the aristocrats—and then add water, reconstituting these classes in the aquatic world and, of course, placing our fish and ourselves on top where we can harvest the blandishments of superior rank. In this respect, I suppose, fishing is less "getting away from it all" than reshuffling the terms to cut ourselves a better deal.

The fish, I hasten to add, know nothing of this.

I don't intend to be snide. I am wholly and happily incriminated, up to my eyebrows in the whole charade which, if nothing else, gives me a good look underwater. In my private echelons of angling, trout rise to the top; for me, no nobler creature swims. And to dissect this predilection exposes the essential capriciousness of it all. I prefer to fish trout, in part, because they take artificial flies readily (though this is equally true of half-a-dozen other species), and I like to fly fish, in part, because it is the way you catch trout. True, the pursuit of trout leads you to beautiful places. But trout also thrive in irrigation ditches and abandoned mining pits, whereas chubs and suckers swim in some of the prettiest water that runs, and I never fish for them (almost never, anyway—of which more later). Because the interplay of streams, trout, plants, and insects is relatively well understood in its overall dynamic, fly fishing offers the sense

that you occupy a universe whose governing principles are at least vaguely scrutable. Yet it is a universe in which whitefish and grayling operate
by the same rules as trout, and in my eyes, these have always been lesser
fish. More exquisitely irrational are the "reasons" I have for elevating the
brown trout above all others. Rainbows are next, brook trout follow, cutthroats last. And among cutthroats, I prefer coastal cutts to Snake River
cutts, and those to the Lahontan strain, and those to the Yellowstone
River variety. After trout, I favor steelhead and salmon, and although
comparatively poor takers of the fly, they still bask in the salmonid
penumbra. They are not trout, but they are troutlike, and that will do.
And so on down the line. It's an elaborate hierarchy, propped only by its
own rickety, internal wherefores, as unsupported by objectivity as it is
unthreatened by it, since all fishermen traffic in the same terms. The current fad for fishing logbooks and hotlines and database software notwithstanding, in the end we are kin to the fennel-eater rather than the
physicist. We espouse our creeds and are apt to revere those who keep
them most faithfully or declaim them the loudest. The holier-than-thou
are a force in all religious affairs, and fly fishing continues to sustain its
sects of purism. The prophet who fishes nothing but dry flies to the
hatch, or 7X tippet, or indigenous trout, somehow seizes the high
ground.

But as an old English professor of mine once said, gently trying to
prod a little sense out of some moronic remark I'd volunteered, "That's
right, but isn't it just a little bit the opposite?" And so it's proven in my
reasonably long association with other fishermen, many of them quite
fine ones. Most are passionate trout or steelhead fishermen, will argue
eloquently about their various chosen species or methods, but have this
in common: Their angling lives were molded from the conviction that
it's infinitely better to be on water than not, and on the water you fish,
and when you fish, you fish for whatever is there. It's not exactly a version of "love the one you're with," because the fact of "fishing" is first.
The fact of the fish is secondary, its particular denomination something
to be dealt with only afterward. I wouldn't go two steps out of my way to
fish for chubs or gar, but I wouldn't go two steps out of my way to avoid
it. Certainly the preoccupation with a single species, like trout, invests

angling with a density and texture of detail that make it less a sport than a world. But beneath it all runs not only the sense that fish, any fish, are deeply fascinating creatures, but the deeper pleasure of being forever caught off guard by the simple fact that there should be fish at all.

In short, when things get lean, I'll go after fish that I normally wouldn't touch with a cattle prod and a tetanus shot. The luckless wino on a bad day panhandling hopefully squeezes a little Sterno for the night; I skulk along the banks in a rubber nose and Groucho-glasses looking for whatever can be made to bite.

Frequently it is whitefish, a poor relation in the trout family. Like catfish, they swim the murky waters between "game fish" and "rough fish." That is, the regulations post bag limits, but they are almost meaninglessly liberal—fifty, a hundred, maybe more. Turnabout is fair play, and if the trout is fishdom's most beautiful inhabitant, the whitefish is its most ludicrous—the forlorn, turned-down mouth; the ill-fitting snout; the tiny, close-set eyes, quizzical and uncomprehending; the face of a man who just missed his bus, of the fish that just doesn't quite get it. It is impossible to take such a face seriously. And although they fight like a zucchini with fins, whitefish take flies readily and thrive in remarkable numbers. In the icy, swollen rivers of March and April, on the Willamette or McKenzie or North Santiam, I fish them, as deadly earnest as any snowbound Montanan with hope in his soul and a mouthful of maggots.

Fishing whitefish, I accidentally learned that suckers will take a fly, a big black stonefly nymph or woolly bugger dragged behind a daunting string of split shot. How a sucker manages to take a fly is anyone's guess. But at times I've cast to them with a rapt and morbid fascination and have caught four different species.

In stillwater oxbows and dead-end backwaters of the big rivers, wolfish packs of squawfish hunt whatever swims, and the efficiency with which they can decimate schools of steelhead and salmon smolts has, in some places, marked them with a price-per-pound bounty. Squawfish have sharp appetites, and I've spent afternoons casting and catching, quitting only when I've pissed away a conscience-worth of good trout flies.

Once, at an old friend's old house on a particularly unattractive slough, I wiled away a few post-party hours well after midnight, fishing chunks of leftover lasagna for gruesome little bullheads, a weak shoulder-shrugging fighter with wicked spines and a slime as nasty as llama spit. I admit to fishing under the influence, but wasn't so drunk that it didn't mean something.

In some sense, these are the acts of a desperate man—even to me—and I can't say I number them among my most cherished angling memories. But they weren't accidental or indiscriminate. There are sometimes holes in curiosity and desire that can be filled only by poking around in the shadowy corners of a thing.

This notion crops up in some surprising places, though they seem less surprising the more fishermen I come to know. A few years ago in a fly shop, I ran into a West Coast angling eminence, a steelhead fisherman and fly tyer of the first stripe. I didn't know him well, and though cordial invitations had been exchanged in the way that anglers do, we'd never fished together. We talked a bit and I asked him had he been fishing and he said, yes, he had, and then took my elbow and led me to a back corner of the shop. In tones at once confidential and offhand, he began telling me about it. It seems he had only just returned from a blistering August week in central Oregon, trout fishing. It had gone badly—car trouble, low water, the heat, fishing that fell far below even his diminished expectations.

On his fifth day out, stubbornly driving to yet another river, he passed a smallish pond in the desert, rimmed with the cracked mud-tiles of receding water. The surface was just boiling with fish, he said, not rising, but rolling and seething with the butter-colored bodies of carp. Without hesitation he strung a rod and headed to the shoreline. Not once, he said, did it ever occur to him not to fish. He threw flies for a while, first streamers, then nymphs, finally dries, managing only to snag and lose one fish.

Reeling in, he knotted on a Hare's Ear and, again without a second thought, coated it in a soft dough made from sandwich bread and pond-water. It took a while to figure out how to cast the thing, and he wanted to be careful, he explained, because he was using a favorite eight-foot Thomas & Thomas cane rod that cost him a little more than $10 an inch.

A slow, lobbing cast did the deed, but when the line hit the water, the ball of dough broke apart. Then with the same systematic specificity he would use to detail a tricky fly dressing, he told me how he first mixed the dough with a little honey, then toothpaste, and finally with peanut butter to get a good adhesive mixture.

The fish were not as easily caught as he thought, though he hooked a few; he made camp there that night and spent the following day adjusting his tackle and methods and eventually catching some fish. In the end, he said, he wasn't much taken with carp as a sport fish, but he'd had a ball and did land one pushing ten pounds.

When he finished the story, he looked at me, shrugged his shoulders, and said, "It's a wiggle," which would sound like an apology to anyone who didn't understand.

There's no point in naming him—the man has a wife and family to look after—or in fact naming any of a dozen other fly-fishing luminaries who have confided similar accounts. For the past few years, I've attended a gathering of what is called the "fly-fishing industry," though its transactions are at least as much social as they are commercial. It draws tackle manufacturers, fly-shop people, fly-fishing noteworthies, writers and other pariahs. In such a collection, there could be but one universal greeting: "Have you been doing any fishing?" And so you get the rundown on trout and salmon, bonefish and dorado, the trips to exotic locales, the familiar and the wonderful. But on an astonishing number of occasions, if you show patience and an open mind, the conversation shades off into the offbeat and weird: stories told, at first with wariness and irony, later with enthusiasm, of alewives on a fly, gar, sheepshead and herring, hardware and bait.

This is fly fishing's dirty little secret, and I find myself invariably drawn to the keepers of it. All other divisions aside, I think in the end there are but two kinds of anglers—those born to fishing and those not. It has nothing to do with expertise or determination or enjoyment. A born fisherman has a soul that wiggles, and though he may be temperamentally inclined to this species or that method, beneath it all is the simple, overriding compulsion to be connected to a fish. If need be, any fish, any way.

My own impulses run pretty much along these lines, and although there are excuses to be made for it, I won't make them. I don't do it to keep "in practice." No claims to the self-conscious delights of forbiddenness, of a cheap-thrills night spent slumming in low-life bars; none of the magazine writer's cheese about the undiscovered sport of secret species— no "diamonds in the rough fish"; no dressing it up to look like more than it is; no farting through silk.

Nor, however, am I the rough beast slouching toward Bozeman. It's a wiggle, no more but nothing less, and though I much prefer the wiggle of the trout to all others, I'll take what I can get without asking if it represents a cruder or a finer sensibility than the purist's. At some level, all fish and fishing, like all gods or powerful emotions or other forms of intoxication, are more alike than not, and it may be that the only difference between a passion and an addiction is the worthiness of its object. I wouldn't know.

6

<hr>

The Farthest Distance
Between Two Points

<hr>

A good traveler has no fixed plans

and is not intent upon arriving.

—*Lao-tzu*, Tao Te Ching

We know by experience it selfe, that it is a

maruelous paine, to finde oute but a short waie,

by long wandering.

—*Roger Ascham,* The Scholemaster

April may indeed be the cruellest month. In the tight tongue-and-groove of the angling year, it seems somehow to have slipped between the cracks. The season seems out of sync with itself. Under warm rains and mild air, the land greens up with promise and propels you forward. But the water holds you back, a brown and roily disappointment, the lagtime of altitude. Some time zones are vertical, and the rivers answer to their origins on mountain peaks still packed in snow, melting with glacial slowness. Remote winters drain into the valley in icy, turbid water, running between grassy banks.

April is a jagged seam, a fault line of the year where the massive plate of winter grinds against the immensity of summer, and the force of occlusion erupts in freak winds, warm deluges, and berserk barometers. The months appear to me as places, fitted like flagstones in a year. Except for April. April is not a place—it is a behavior, the irascible shucking of an itchy skin.

Last month's clocklike hatches of March Browns on the big valley rivers have wound down and with them the first foretaste of a summer's dry-fly fishing. Now you might fish all afternoon for a small flurry of mayflies that comes and goes in fifteen minutes and a rise of trout that lasts half as long. Just as often, there's nothing at all. Still six weeks away, the Deschutes stonefly hatch is just beyond the range of fruitful anticipation. The winter steelhead have spawned and gone and the first swell of summer fish is just now gathering off the coast. A few shad have arrived, but not yet in numbers worth troubling about. You can cobble together only odds and ends: a few hours nymphing whitefish; casting at midnight off jetties on the coast for black rockfish; taking a beating in the afternoon surf, fishing perch; half a morning indulging the eternal vanity of taking a spring chinook on a fly. But it's hard to find a mainstay in these acrobatics. They don't even feel much like fishing, just something to do with your hands.

This year is especially bad. The El Niño Current in the Pacific made for an unusually mild winter, bringing balmy air and relatively little rain. The rivers, ordinarily swollen beyond hope, remained perfectly fishable, and the fishing was exceptional. Though trout season closes in winter, taking whitefish is still permitted, and this technicality gives rise to a benign annual charade in which the serious fly fisherman breaks out his tackle and takes to the water. He'll catch trout after trout for hours, pretending to astonishment and disappointment that they are not whitefish, while the Fish and Wildlife people pretend to believe him. The deception is harmless enough, and this year it went on and on.

In April, the party was raided. The year caught up with itself and stalled out in a series of storm systems over the Pacific. On the nightly satellite photos, thick spirals of clouds like Crab Nebulae squatted on the Gulf of Alaska, spinning slowly counterclockwise, wheeling the year back to winter and sweeping wave after wave of December weather over the coast and valley.

Driven indoors, I tied flies by the pound, tore down reels and oiled them, built leaders, cleaned out my vest, patched waders, and organized my rods (first by length, then line size, and finally by degrees of affection). I spent a couple weeks in this methadone fishing, a substitute less important for what it does than for what it prevents from happening. Outside my window, a white camellia bloomed feebly, and from a rusted gutter left unrepaired during sea-run cutthroat season, rain leaked down to a concrete block and tapped impatiently. Having only so much tackle to fuss with, I eventually tinkered myself into a corner—all dressed up and no place to go.

But at certain times, in certain moods, it simply feels better to be moving than standing still. And rather than go no place, I decided to go no place in particular, on the kind of trip defined only by its impelling energy. You don't go somewhere, you just go. Instead of seeking a place that conforms to the shape of your desire, you allow desire to shape itself around whatever places happen to present themselves.

After a winter of good fishing, focused tightly on a few stretches of a few rivers, April came as an abrupt dislocation, and primed me for just such a trip. In a season when everything rejuvenates by taking root, there can be a kind of renewal in rootlessness too. The novelist Don DeLillo once observed, "Plots carry their own logic. There is a tendency of plots to move toward death." Plans and plots are inertial, with an order and direction governed by the inexorable gravity of an endpoint. They imply patterns of inevitability which, from forceps to headstone, are the shortest distance between two points. The kind of trip I had in mind, on the other hand—unprescribed, directionless, and entropic—is the farthest.

If just about anywhere is possible, just about anything may be necessary. I packed up trout rods from 3- to 6-weight and a vest with everything from big streamers to midges. The prospect of lake fishing occurred to me, and I tossed in another rod, a long 7-weight; a few reels with assorted sinking lines; a float tube and fins; a pump to blow it up. There was a separate vest, a rod, and two reels for steelhead, along with a wading staff and cleats. Rain gear, a fly-tying kit, extra flies, hatch books, neoprene waders and lightweight ones, and boots. On impulse, I added a huge eleven-and-a-half-foot surf rod and a big spinning reel to the growing pile, and then took them out. No point in overdoing it.

I headed north for the simple reason that the nearest gas station lay in that direction. Along the highway, I began seeing unusual numbers of hawks and counted eleven of them in less than ten miles, perched on fence-posts, utility poles, and billboards, hunched against the drizzle. Sometimes it's hard not to look for omens and signs. My knowledge of birds is only middling, but I knew at once these were rough-legged hawks. I'd seen them featured in countless miles of raptor footage that aired on public television in the last decade, when legions of sleekly groomed Reagan-youth fueled a national fascination with handsome predators. I weighed the various interpretations of the omen, inconclusively.

When I began to hit the Portland traffic, I veered east toward the mountains, and eventually stopped some time later at a sagging little diner near the Clackamas River for coffee and information. Behind the counter, tiny red lights flashed silently in sequence on a police scanner, and an amber power lamp glowed on the front of a CB base unit. The only sound, however, issued from the tinny speaker of a transistor radio hung on a nail, a drone I recognized at once as the National Weather Service broadcast. Parked on a counter stool, an aged waitress in a peach uniform and white Adidas poured coffee without getting up. The fishing was slow, she said, "maybe some winter fish below the dam." She put on a pair of half-moon reading glasses and leaned over to a handwritten chart taped to the cash register.

"Six-point-three feet. That's last night. Radio man," she nodded vaguely behind her, "says more weather's moving in. River's blowed out as it is. Get caught in that and you won't stop floatin' till the Japs fish you out." She looked meaningfully over the tops of her glasses, "A Jap'll eat fish eyes, you know."

I drove to see the river anyway. It was empty except for two bait plunkers huddled like a pair of hams by a damp, smoky fire. I watched for a time, waiting for something in the scene to lure me past the effort of unpacking my gear, and in the end moved higher up the river, away from any fishing. The season closed here three weeks ago, but there were fish in the river. Getting out to stretch my legs, I walked along a little tributary and found a pair of spawning steelhead, finning over the gravel, looking bushed. Disjunctions in scale have a way of magnifying things that is rare in the natural world, and the sight of big fish in small water is a magnetic spectacle. You couldn't help but wonder how, through the gauntlet of seals, gill nets, dams, and fishermen, they ever made it up here, if they were somehow better than other fish or just got the breaks.

Their stretch of holding water was formed by a beaver dam, which is what first caught my attention. Some years ago, I spent part of a day on a spawning tributary of a coastal river, tearing apart logjams and beaver dams that, in those less-enlightened times, were presumed to inhibit the upstream passage of fish. Even a small beaver dam is a remarkably tough structure and can take two men an hour to dislodge. What struck me most, though, was not how strongly they were built, but how they were started in the first place. This one was typical—on the bank, I counted eleven smallish Douglas fir stumps, each rising from a pile of cuttings, the fallen trunks scattered randomly on the forest floor. Some fell away from the stream, some parallel to its banks, others with the uppermost branches just touching the water. Each was a shot in the dark and a clean miss. Apparently, the eleventh one at last fell across to the other bank and got things moving. The much vaunted efficiency of nature's little creatures notwithstanding, the beavers, like the pair of steelhead, just plugged away, played like they knew how, and waited for lucky accidents—a fallen tree to start a dam, a dam to make a little spawning run, a guy who hadn't come to ruin them both. It occurred to me only later that my own method was not substantially different.

The radio man, as it turned out, didn't lie. Late in the day, a squall-like storm moved in, dropping sheets of rain that turned to clots of heavy, wet snow near Blue Box Pass, and finally thinned to a drizzle east of the Cascades when I pulled into Maupin at nightfall.

Flanking the Deschutes River, Maupin is the last major boat landing before the near-certain fatality of Sherars Falls. In six weeks, the first packs of summer rafters would arrive and the town would come alive, renting equipment, selling beer and groceries, frying burgers, running shuttles, and generally laying on some fat against the long, unprosperous winter. But now, in April, the place just waited, lean, vacant, and cheerless. Some time during the night, the rain stopped. I fished an hour in the raw, wintry morning, and left.

You don't take a trip like this. It takes you. It is indeterminate, open-ended, almost a succession of tangents except that there is no main line of navigation and so nothing is really tangential. A small body in space, I understand—an asteroid, a meteor, a particle of dust—may travel in just this way. Drawn by some distant star or planet, it bends around the gravitational field, and momentum carries it in a new direction, toward some other star or planet that diverts it yet again. A chunk of matter zigzags through space in a trajectory largely defined by things other than itself. There is, at certain times, the same inertness to being, when what you sense most clearly are the currents outside yourself, shifting forces of uncertain direction. And in such moments, what's needed most is to throw up a sail, pull in the keelboard, and just see where the drift takes you.

Still, traveling like this with no destination and no steam of your own takes some getting used to. It is difficult not to look ahead, not to see yourself on the way to somewhere. The whole thrust bucks a lifetime of habit by inverting the accustomed relation of destination and desire. Even temporary dislocations are unsettling—which is exactly why they're good for you—and for the first few days, I reluctantly picked at the trip like a plate of existential vegetables. I missed my wife, worried about the weather, about work left undone, about where to go next.

My notes record only fragments. Half a sentence for a river, a highway in an aside, a parenthetical stopping place. Spot-fishing the John Day River for hungry eight-inch smallmouth. Up the gulches and dry washes near Dayville, hunting for thunder-egg geodes. On the Crooked River, a handful of aquatic weeds squirming with hundreds of shrimplike scuds, a tantalizing fact I was unable to translate into trout. And driving, long, long, textureless miles of greening desert. All of these felt somehow preliminary. I waited, bored by my own company, and considered turning back. There seemed to be no point, which was true, and was also precisely the point.

But unpatterned time and routineless days tug at you with a sly, seductive insistence; bit by bit, they persuade you to themselves and begin to win you over. The ordinary formulae of daily life give way to pleasantly odd private jags, eating when the mood strikes, sleeping when it suits you, fishing or not, abruptly deciding to move on or content to linger, keeping irregular hours. I stopped taking notes. As always, change began with the rivers. Strangely (or not so strangely as I discovered later), I ran into no other fishermen over the course of nearly a week. I could work the best water without hurry, move when I wished, humor any whim of technique or method, and generally indulge the luxury of a man who has a trout stream entirely to himself. Inevitably, the tone and timbre of the fishing rippled back into the trip and subsumed it. According to Jung, crossing a river represents a fundamental change of attitude. Pity he didn't fish; he would have recognized that rivers are far more powerful as agents of transformation than symbols for it.

The turning point came one day along the Deschutes. I'm still not quite sure what led me back there—habit, accident, the simple consequence of unchecked momentum. I just found myself there one overcast afternoon standing on Lower Bridge, seventy-five miles above Maupin, scanning the water for rises. Against the cattails and willow thickets, a few trout dimpled sporadically. In late winter, big browns feed on the surface, first to a hatch of small black stoneflies and, later, March Browns. The odds of hitting a fish four pounds or better on a dry fly suddenly fall into betting range. But in a place like this, I care less for the stakes than for the game, for sight-fishing to individual risers on glassy, unforgiving currents. So I whittled an afternoon down to evening, sitting on the banks, marking rises, and fishing among flooded tule and current-swept brush to shy, jittery trout, one at a time.

This is a tough, technical kind of fishing, careful, deliberate, and intensely absorbing; that I'm not very good at it doesn't diminish its particular satisfactions. In fishing (among other things) style and technique are important only insofar as they define the shape of one's appreciation. Alter the style, and you change as well the nature of your pleasure. In blind fishing, for instance, say in searching a riffle with a floating fly or nymphing pocket water, you prospect for the unknown, wondering always where the trout might lie, what fly might tempt it, what cast it might come on. You fish, in essence, for surprise out of nowhere, for an instant in which you suddenly become aware that you're attached to a heartbeat. Fishing a heavy hatch—in most other respects the antithesis of blind-casting—nonetheless holds much the same appeal. I think it's fair to say that most anglers are apt to flock shoot a good rise of fish, picking out a density of rings, dropping a fly in the middle of them, and trusting to the numbers. Here, too, we fish for that moment of uncertainty, that tiny interval of unresolvedness in which we strain to assess just what it is we have hold of, how big it might be, and what will happen next. As in blind fishing, much of the thrill lies in seeing what you come up with.

But the deliberate, studied fishing to a single rising trout reverses the circumstances and kindles an altogether different type of engagement. Here, the fish is the given. You know its precise location, the form and pattern of rises, often the size, and quite possibly the insect it's feeding on. With the endpoint defined, getting there becomes the question. From the particularities there emerges a kind of abstract problem, almost geometric in design—a calculation of drift lines, curve casts, and angles of presentation, superimposed on the tempo of the rise, and predicated on the caginess of your own surmise. Alternatives must be weighed; small adaptations undertaken; adjustments made one at a time; a solution converged upon; and, sometimes, the final luxury of knowing exactly when you got it right. You want to catch the fish, but you want more to figure it out, and the particular satisfactions stem less from the eventuality than the process by which the whole thing unfolds.

I doubt that I cast to more than ten or twelve fish that day and hooked only a few of them. But I did, at last, catch the rhythm of the trip.

From the road map, Bend, Oregon, rose up as an enormous hot shower. Finding one proved little trouble. Once an unassuming little town at the edge of the desert, Bend suffered the irreparable misfortune, some years back, of being "discovered." Now it sprawls in random ugliness, a casualty of too much money too fast. The old center of town is ringed with low-slung motels, fast-food huts, strange extraterrestrial boutiques, minimalls, and inflatable subdivisions, and overall, looks like something you might find if Dante had been a real estate developer. I had plenty of opportunity to see it all, touring the place two or three times when I got lost looking for a fly shop. It turned out to be three blocks from the motel.

I needed only some tippet material, which I asked for in a strange glottal croak, far too loud and edged with the faint inflection of hysteria. For the past six days, it suddenly occurred to me, I hadn't spoken to a soul. I also discovered something else—general trout season had opened only the day before. In a number of places, I'd unknowingly fished on closed water, which went a long way toward explaining why I'd seen no one else. This doesn't seem the kind of detail that's easily overlooked, but if you habitually fly fish with barbless hooks and release all your trout— that is, uniformly abide by the most restrictive legal provisions—you get remarkably cavalier about matters like size and bag limits, and sometimes seasons, because they so rarely impinge on your fishing. In most cases, you're already doing far more than the law requires, and in time it comes to seem impossible that you could do anything illegal. Then, too, I suppose, deep down you hang from that last, shady loophole—to claim you're after whitefish—though only an angler with the soul of a personal-injury lawyer could trot this out with any conviction.

I should have been relieved at not being caught; instead I felt only like an idiot—a lucky idiot at that, which is the most ridiculous kind. I'd hoped to summon the spirit of Thoreau in the Maine woods or Pirsig on his motorcycle. Instead I got Mister Magoo.

I told the fly-shop clerk nothing of this and made only the usual inquiries. He said that the fishing had been "only fair," a revelation that surprised me. A fly shop is the only place I know of where the fishing is always "excellent," since there's no reason to provide a customer with less than best. As a result, any fly-shop report must be adjusted for inflation, which in this case meant fishing was lousy. We talked a bit, he suggesting a few places I might try, when our conversation drew the attention of a customer who seemed to browse the shop solely for this opportunity. He leaned an elbow on the glass counter, beamed an indulgent smile, and introduced himself: "Can I tell you a little something about fly fishing?" Statistically, my chances of running into someone who can "tell me a little something about fly fishing" are pretty good, so I had to wonder how this person so soundly whipped the odds. The type is regrettably familiar—polar fleece and a haircut stretched over a hideous bubble of gas. They never brag. It is too merciful. Instead, they insist upon "explaining" things to you, benevolently strolling among the worldlings and torturing them with little lectures. This one was particularly insufferable, droning at length about the previous weekend spent on a two-hundred-dollar-a-day fee-lake, hitting fish after fish on midges, modestly subordinating his own Olympian achievements to more general proclamations on the proper way to fish *Chironomids* on still water and play large trout on light tippets. It was amply clear that his actual knowledge of midge fishing was dwarfed even by my own pale understanding of the subject. Worst of all, he repeatedly referred to the insects as "Geronimos," and each authoritative mispronunciation seemed like a tiny pellet expelled solely for my irritation. I left, and forgot my tippet material.

But it's an ill windbag that blows nobody any good, and if nothing else, he did remind me about stillwater fishing, which is sometimes obscured by my overly rigid association of trout with rivers. The fee-lake held little attraction. I still carry around enough populist baggage to be put off by the idea of paying to fish. The overtones of elitism don't bother me so much (after all, *not* paying for fishing is perhaps itself a form of elitism). Rather, fee-fishing seems somehow rigged, artificial, too contrary to the spirit of the thing. It's commonly remarked among many anglers (particularly those who can't afford it) that paying for fishing—not for tackle, or travel, or licenses, but simply for someone's consent—is a lot like paying for sex. Ethics aside, such arrangements, businesslike as they may be, nonetheless hinge on a pretty unflattering species of indolence. But in a world steaming full-throttle toward privatization, this attitude may eventually become a little too precious.

I left Bend in a pounding rainstorm, looping southeast toward drier skies (which I eventually caught up with) and a rumored pond (which I never found). Another day and a half of continuous prospecting turned up nothing, and I was well into the second of the truck's two twenty-three-gallon fuel tanks. In the eerie moonscape of the Warner Valley, I spread a map on the dust and pinned the corners with rocks. Unchecked, the prevailing momentum would bring me south to Pyramid Lake in

Nevada by the next day. The road to the nearest gas station ran north. I debated, then took it.

There's little to say about long drives that hasn't already been said. They dislocate your sense of reality, and the outside world becomes less a place than a medium through which you vaguely move. Whatever is real is contained within the jarring shell of a pickup cab, and the landscape rolls by like a long, plotless movie projected from all sides. After a while, you can't remember a time when you weren't driving, and what you might have seen or done seem like things told to you by someone else.

More than anything, though, is the weird introspection that it induces. On a small tape recorder, I started taking notes again. I dictated replies to long-neglected correspondence, made lists of various kinds, pondered out loud the big questions. I composed a letter of resignation from my job, a churlish and huffy little speech (never delivered) that trailed off into a rambling indictment of the American university, which gleefully split the atom while solemnly guarding the integrity of the infinitive. For a time, I just let the tape run—recording the road vibration and wind noise, the gargle of a perforated exhaust, John Hiatt singing about a band of Indians—to remind me of the traveling (I am listening to it now). Seized by some morbidity, I made out my will.

The gas station at Brothers came just in time, right at the point when it occurred to me that I wasn't really taking notes. I was talking to myself. In a dingy little restroom, I stripped to the waist, washed up in the sink and shaved, and got my bearings again. Half an hour away lay a small reservoir I'd heard about. An astonishing number of these impoundments are scattered about this arid, unremittingly exposed landscape. People call them "lakes," though this is an insult to real lakes everywhere. Most are manmade, little more than shallow depressions with a bulldozed earthen dam just high enough to trap a thin film of turbid, ugly water. Some are seasonal, some more or less permanent, and of those, a few manage one deeply redeeming quality—they grow trout at a phenomenal rate. The one I made camp on had this reputation.

In the morning, for the first time since setting out, the sun rose in a cloudless sky. It woke me early. A few fishermen were already on the water; offshore, a guy in a float tube netted a trout. I raised my rod and pointed with exaggerated gestures at the fly on my hook keeper. He cupped a hand to his mouth and shouted, "Nimps!" I walked on, led much of the way by a horned lark hopping through sagebrush in a highly convincing crippled-wing performance. On a small arm of the lake where I could get the morning sun to my back and the glare from my eyes, I tried nimp after nimp. Big dragonfly nymphs on sink-tips, olive marabou damsels on intermediate lines, and finally, by luck, a floating line and a #14 Prince. That one rang the bell.

In a rare inversion of the normal order, the catching was comparatively brisk, although the fishing itself was slow. I made maybe twenty casts an hour. There was the long delivery, an even longer pause to let the fly sink, followed by an agonizingly deliberate, inching retrieve almost to the rod tip. Then, just the smallest resistance. Not a tug, only the faint feeling of a little extra weight. I missed the first few fish, assuming that the take would be more decisive and palpable, but eventually got the hang of it. None of the trout jumped; in the cold water, they dogged the bottom amid the flooded sagebrush; by noon, I'd taken seven thick rainbows, and lost as many more.

The fishing held up well for the next couple of days, predictable enough to require only a single box of flies and a minimum of gear. One morning, I set about emptying my vest of extraneous baggage (of which there was an enormous quantity). I have never quite made peace with my vest and envy the angler for whom it is a settled matter. He may try a new gadget here or there, or carry a few new fly patterns now and then, but for the most part the character, the gestalt of the vest is a formed and recognizable thing. My own vest, though, has always been restless and dynamic, a pendulum oscillating between a profligate Neronian excess that knows no limits and a lean Spartanism that admits no frills. My flyfishing life, in fact, has wandered between these same extremes, at times reflecting the conviction that the world is entirely contingent and is best met by covering all the bases. Gradually this gives way to its opposite— trusting to a few wisely chosen things and recognizing that a larger number of alternatives merely increases the likelihood, in any given circumstance, of resorting to the wrong one. Although a rod or reel may embody a general taste, or specific predilection, or even an aesthetic, it is finally just a piece of gear. But a vest is a philosophy, and paring mine down was overdue.

The weather continued to moderate—cool, sunny days, cold and clear nights—and time passed in the kind of pleasant rhythm that comes easily when you are alone. Yet at the same time I became aware again of a vague feeling I'd had off and on since the beginning. It was more inkling than idea, a vague perception that something was hovering on the perimeter of this trip. I sensed it only as an indistinct significance, possibly a place or a direction, something to find or be found by, or perhaps only a reason for coming. It didn't drive the trip, but seemed to accumulate along with it, and though I now understand what it was, at the time it remained at the edge of intuition and would not be thought or coaxed into the open, or snuck up on and surprised. Nor would it quite go away.

The trip through Hines was a strange hallucination. A gas station attendant discovered a grotesque swelling on the sidewall of a rear tire. I was sent to a specialist who diagnosed the bulge as terminal, indicating as well that the other tire, to all appearances in good health, was in fact rapidly failing. Skeptical but helpless, I surrendered the keys and walked a few blocks to a diner. For reasons that became abundantly clear, it announced itself with a handlettered sign—no name, just a message: "The Worst Food in Oregon." This, I discovered, was no joke. The coffee might just have been the worst in the world. I ordered up the breakfast special (recorded in my notes as "Toast-and-Eggs Regret"), and under the circumstances, found it difficult to complain about the result, the cook having lived up so fully to his end of the agreement. The place itself was scarcely larger than a Fotomat, with a few picnic tables inside, and walls covered in graffiti of a spooky and unvarying "Go Jesus!" type. The management apparently encouraged the practice, which seemed appropriate to an establishment where mere matters of the flesh, like food, commanded so little regard.

Outside the tire dealer, my pickup awaited as promised. I paid the bill, and the clerk handed over a receipt along with a package wrapped neatly in white paper and hard as a brick, a promotional bonus, I was told, for the new radials. I asked what was in it. "Seven pounds of ground beef," he said, walking off. One might have expected a stainless-steel tire gauge or a Naugahyde litter bag. Instead, burger—the national solvent. Only in America.

It wasn't over. A few miles from town, I pulled into one of those convenience market/hardware store/gas station/bait shop/video rental places, the kind of fully self-contained retail ecosystem that flourishes only in thinly populated areas. I hoped to get some information about the fishing. The clerk was pleasant, an inexhaustible talker more than eager to help. In the course of a few minutes, he found out where I was from—he had people there—and established to his satisfaction that although we had no friends in common, his friends almost certainly knew my friends, which made us friends of a sort. The discovery pleased him enormously, for he was bursting with some news about the fishing, but obviously regarded the intelligence as so valuable that he wouldn't want it to fall into the wrong hands, and by god wasn't it lucky and *pretty incredible* to boot that such a good friend should happen by because he just had to tell *somebody*.

He drew close, took a quick glance around the empty shop just to be safe, and addressed me in tones I hadn't heard since *The Graduate*. Dustin Hoffman got one word: "Plastics." I got four—*Pautzke's Balls of Fire*.

My face must have betrayed the meaninglessness of this revelation, and so he launched into a light-speed paean to the Balls of Fire as I listened impatiently for more specific information about what I concluded must be some very local fly pattern and, of course, waited for him to produce a Ball of Fire for my inspection.

The truth dawned gradually. After each invocation of the name, he gestured vaguely behind him, where my eyes finally rested on several rows of glass jars entombing garishly dyed individual salmon eggs—hot orange, electric red, neon pink—each bottle burning a hundred eternal flames in the memory of Pautzke.

The clerk would not be reined in. He explicated the theory of the Balls of Fire, furnished corroborating examples of their efficacy, and moved on to discourse in general about the genius of Pautzke. I interrupted to ask him if the pink ones tasted any different from the orange ones or if it was just a matter of color. He paused for the first time, conceded it was an interesting question that he couldn't answer, but assured me it could not have escaped the notice of one such as Pautzke and that the whole matter had undoubtedly been worked out.

The entire exchange—edited substantially for brevity—took place less than two feet from a plastic display case housing several hundred reasonably decent trout flies. Of these, the clerk never once made mention even when I reminded him that I would be fly fishing, a comment that met with a second pause, as though he were trying to determine any conceivable relevance of my remark to the Balls of Fire. He apparently concluded there was none, and though I declined his offers, we parted friends, sensing perhaps some deeper kinship.

An hour south, the Steens first appeared, an isolated mountain range in remote country riven with geological fault lines. Ten million years ago, the area was a broad basalt plateau; over time, stresses along the faults fractured the sheet of rock into immense blocks. Some of the blocks sank, like the ones to the east in the Alvord Valley. Others pushed upward in abrupt, sheared escarpments, forming the Steens that rise a mile above the valley floor and 10,000 feet above sea level. The western approach to the Steens rim, near Frenchglen, is a gradual rise, cut intermittently by deep glacial valleys. At the foot of the mountains runs the Blitzen River. Moving water again.

The Blitzen, I've been told repeatedly, holds some large rainbows, though I've never hooked one or seen one or been in the presence of anyone who has. Rumors take on a life of their own whenever big fish are involved. But it is a hard, jagged, beautiful place, and in past years I've hiked upstream for the small native redbands, a subspecies of rainbow trout that long ago adapted to the desert. Mostly, they inhabit the steep canyon of the upper river, and I wouldn't go there on this trip. The jeep trail is tenuous enough in the best weather; at this time of year, it would be five miles of thigh-deep mudholes.

I worked the lower river, where it levels out onto a marshy plain that, in a month or so, would breed a quantity of mosquitoes impossible to believe in this dry landscape. Again, only the small fish were willing, though plenty of those.

Nothing gnaws like a detail, and comfortably encamped with fishing enough to satisfy, I became strangely consumed with the burger question. A windfall, even a small one, is not to be taken lightly. Thawing in the cooler, the package had bled on the beer and stained the water a thin, milky pink. I weighed the options against its obviously accelerating half-life, and the next night mashed the whole lump into a big cast-iron skillet over a white-gas stove, and for the better part of an hour tended the largest hamburger with which I've ever personally come into contact. Out of duty, I ate as much as I could, wrapped a few cold wedges in a plastic bag, and laid the remainder on a stump near camp. In the morning it was gone, a second windfall for some other creature and an occasion for musing: a bad tire was transformed into a hunk of ground beef, which in turn became a skunk or porcupine, which might eventually meet its own fate beneath a careless tire. "Burger to burger, dust to dust." Clearly, it was time to move on.

Down the Catlow Valley, the flatland was already greening and the hillside sprouted shoots of monkey flower that would soon line the seeps and springs with their absurdly pure yellow flowers. On the long grade between the Steens and Pueblos, I coasted into Fields and another one of the oddest little eateries on the planet, a low-ceilinged white-enamel cubicle, like the inside of a refrigerator, heavy with the smell of grilling hamburgers. I ordered the fish.

By early evening I was headed back north on the Fields-Denio Road, a fifty-mile stretch of washboard gravel that follows the eastern base of the Steens. Twenty minutes out of Fields, I stopped at a hot springs that bubbled through fissures in the hillside. Someone, some time ago, had cozied it up with a cement basin and a corrugated steel windbreak, and it's become a regular stopping point for the few travelers on this road. Sitting and soaking, I watched the water steam in the cool air and trickle down to the Alvord Desert spread out before me, sixty square miles of dust, sand, and baked dirt, flat as a griddle and almost completely devoid of vegetation. Over the desert floor, columns of soil swirled in dust devils, coalescing suddenly, traveling a random spin over the flats, and settling back into powder when the wind quieted.

With the mountains to your back and Tule Springs Rim on the far side of the valley, you get the distinct and accurate impression that you're sitting at the bottom of a lake. By the time of the last ice age, the Alvord Basin was filled with water, forming a lake nearly a hundred miles long, though still dwarfed by the huge inland seas of Lake Bonneville and Lake Lahontan to the south. Long cut off from any connection with other waters, the cutthroat in the Alvord Basin evolved into a distinct subspecies that, like the redband, adapted to tolerate the increasingly harsh conditions of the region—burning cold winters; frigid runoff; the splintering heat of high summer; streams that almost disappear in rainless spells; and warm slackwater creeks so saturated with dissolved minerals that the water leaves a white film on waders when it evaporates.

About 8,000 years ago, the lake dried up completely and the trout retreated to the small mountain streams, their numbers dwindling until, in this century, they were thought to have become extinct. In spite of their evolutionary handstands, the cutthroats couldn't compete with cattle herds and irrigators for habitat and were too willing to interbreed with introduced trout to maintain an undiluted wild gene pool. But in recent years, a handful of fish believed to be the Alvord strain were discovered toughing it out in a remote creek, a remarkable fact that holds only the grimmest reassurances.

But this ancient lakebed validates the overwhelming sense of this desert as a world of its own. Even now, the streams that head in the mountains are part of no larger river system. Willow Creek, Whitehorse Creek, Trout Creek, Indian, Pike, and Alvord Creeks are their own watersheds. They simply flow out of the mountains to a dish in the dust, as if nothing had changed in 10,000 years, though now the waters simply sink into nothingness or evaporate in alkaline sumps. Few sights can affect a fisherman more profoundly than to walk downstream along one of these creeks and watch it, in just a few yards, disappear into the desert floor. You know you are in a different place, self-enclosed, with its own rules.

As always, some people just don't get it. One morning, a few years back, the handful of residents here awoke to find an enormous geometric design carved into the hard desert flat. It immediately occasioned the usual titillating speculation about extra-terrestrial beings that, in the twentieth century, have become technology's way of accommodating the persistent human need for a metaphysic. I strongly suspect that should such a visitation ever occur, it would run a disappointing second to the expectation, like meeting the Buddha and discovering he had hemorrhoids and a short temper. On the other hand, no spacemen have so far appeared, which at least argues for superior intelligence.

As it turned out, a certain "artist" stepped forward to take credit for the design, explaining that when no one was looking (which could be almost any time out here), he and a few accomplices laid out the pattern with stakes and string and harrowed it into the dirt with a hand plow. The figure, he patiently elaborated, reproduced an ancient, mystical pattern, meditating upon which would heal the aura, grow hair on a bald soul, cure existential dyspepsia, and administer karmic medicaments of various sorts, of which a misty, Miss America-like version of peace on earth was the very least to be expected.

In an unrelated incident, Bill Witherspoon, a name terminally associated with frauds of this type, erected a similar monument to himself—several hundred three-story logs stuck upright over sixty acres of desert to form a "cosmic transducer." (It is my great hope that a real visionary will come along and plant a giant, stuffed coyote by each pole, a hind leg lifted in salute to Witherspoon's achievement.) The cosmic transducer was erected, he said, to make contact with nature, because "to make contact with nature is to make contact with the most intimate part of oneself." Personally, I prefer that he just went somewhere in private and made contact with the most intimate part of himself in an essentially similar, but less obtrusive, fashion. The arrogance and obtuseness of spirit are staggering, as though the place somehow needed these portraits of the artist to invest it with significance.

It was after dark when I pulled off on the rutted two-track leading to Mann Lake. I made camp in the light of a half-moon. Despite the clear sky, the surest sign of a cold night in the desert, the air was inexplicably mild.

At certain moments, this can be a deeply serene place, one of those landscapes in which you feel a kind of reparative and healing power, even when you don't believe yourself to be in need of these things. In part, I think, it is a consequence of perspective. To the west, two miles off but feeling much closer, the white peaks of the Steens rise a mile high. In saddles between angular summits, snow and ice linger into summer. Below them, the mountains fall away in a steep, smooth arc, sloping more gradually at the foot, and finally leveling down to the shore of the lake, forming one of the most beautiful curves of landscape I've ever seen. The scale is impossible to hold out against; the land coaxes you into a kind of equilibrium with itself.

At other times, however, it simply beats you into submission, and five or six days out here can leave you feeling pretty worked over. The high-summer sun will simmer your brain in its own juice, and there is no shade anywhere; in winter, eyes ache from the cold and the hair in your nose crackles like icicles. The distance from one extreme to the other is sometimes a matter of minutes. With mountains so close on the west, you can never see the change coming. The weather is on top of you in an instant. I've fished the far shore of the lake in shirtsleeves, bolted for camp when I felt the first waves of cold air rolling down the mountain, and jogged the last hundred yards in snow.

Mostly, it's the wind, the most difficult element to convey because people think they understand it already. They know windy days and believe they can imagine one after another after another. Yet they still have no idea of a place where the wind doesn't die down, not at evening, not in early morning. It rocks a tent all night long. There is nothing to block or blunt the incessant tunnel of moving air and all that goes with it—alkali dust, cinders, bits of dry grass and sage bark; the lip-cracking dryness; and perhaps in the end, most inescapable of all, the noise rushing ceaselessly past your ears like traffic, so unremitting that it finally seems to be coming from inside your head.

On a windy afternoon, every angler on the lake will be lined up on the lee shore, hunched against the weather, with forty feet of fly line held stiffly horizontal over the water. You must dip the rod tip in the lake to set down a fly. And most of the fish are on the other side of the lake anyway, feeding on the drift and churn of the windward shore.

Still, it can be worth the trouble. The Lahontan cutthroats here— another ice-age subspecies genetically groomed for desert life—are remarkably handsome fish and grow to a size that seems impossible in this thin pan of water. They can sometimes be caught on big woolly buggers or leeches, sometimes on damsel or *Callibaetis* nymphs, sometimes on nothing at all. Day-in and day-out, though, the staple is *Chironomid* pupae, midges, Geronimos. They flourish here in unimaginable abundance, and on a warm summer evening, enormous numbers of adults collect along the shore, swarming about, clinging to grasses or to one another, vibrating in the wind. From some distance away, you can hear their collective sound, a continuous low-level whine, everywhere in general but nowhere in particular, nearly subsonic, like the hum of a power plant.

When I finished making camp, I walked down to the lake and there, for the first time, noticed something strange. There was no wind. It was absolutely still.

There is, I'm convinced, an innate human predisposition toward pattern-making. From three random dots on a blank page, the mind's eye constructs a triangle. We find familiar outlines in the night sky and transform clouds into recognizable shapes. We discern as well geometries of experience and order them in narrative. History, to us, has a structure and we read it like a long, untidy novel. Our own life stretches behind us as a story told, and ahead like a plot unfolding around a hero named after ourselves.

At home in the Willamette Valley, looking back on the trip and tracing on a map where I'd been, I saw just such a pattern unexpectedly emerge from a route that seemed at the time shapeless and undesigned. Though I had deliberately taken a trip with no particular direction, it now seemed to have a particular indirection, which can be just as certain, and sometimes truer. I'd driven wide, looping curves, wandering back and forth, zigzagging across a hypothetical line that marked the shortest distance from my doorstep to the shore of Mann Lake. And whether drawn or impelled, I still can't say.

That first morning I awoke, about as far away from home as I could get and still find trout, in a landscape as capricious and as little to be counted on as any I know, and discovered what couldn't be seen the night before. A vast expanse of purple lupine on the desert floor tinted the landscape with a deep amethyst, cupped between broken ridges. The air, still calm, was spiced with the odor of rabbitbrush blooming in a million tiny yellow blossoms. Bees worked the morning nectar flow, and the calls of meadowlarks chimed off the rimrock. And I remember standing there and thinking that back home in the valley, it must be spring now, too.

7

Stoned Again

No, it was too much. The line between madness

and masochism was already hazy. . . .

—*Hunter Thompson*, Fear and Loathing in Las Vegas

"The essence of wisdom," fishing partner Bill Potts remarked, yanking his second consecutive cast out of an alder crown, "is in knowing that if you make a mistake, you'll make it again." For some reason, this notion recurs in my life as a kind of existential refrain. My father, a gifted woodworker among many other things, rendered his own version from plane shavings and sawdust. "I cut it off twice," he'd say looking up at me, a few ashes from his pipe drifting down to the piece of lumber in his hand, "and it's still too short." I've always interpreted these as warnings and have not been disappointed.

Every year in that brief interval when spring has ended and summer not quite begun, my better judgment and I take separate vacations. It wanders off for points unknown, while I head once again to the Deschutes River.

The Deschutes, or the forty-five-mile stretch of it between Warm Springs and Maupin, is my home water, though it isn't particularly close to home and not the river I fish most often. Nor does the river even approximate my Platonic trout stream. The size and depth, the forbidding velocity of the current, the sheer volume of water, all exceed the proportions of comfortable imagining, and much of what is there seems beyond reach or rapport. You can become familiar with the river, but it defies the intimacy of my ideal. Yet the place is magnetic for precisely this reason: It confronts you with your own incapacity to know.

The landscape here is an acutely sensed contradiction. In the geographical abridgments we so often trade in, Oregon is condensed to a lush, misty tract of Douglas fir and cedar, shrouding the Pacific coast. But in the original unexpurgated edition, there is a portion of the state (a very large portion) that lies to the east of the Cascade Mountains. Most of it is arid territory, and much of that is desert—not the sand-and-saguaro of Sonora, but harsh and brittle expanses of sage, rabbitbrush, cheatgrass, and juniper tenuously anchored in twenty million acres of windblown volcanic dust that settles in a gritty film on your teeth. And through the middle of it flows a hundred miles of some of the richest trout water west of Montana. It took some thirty-five thousand centuries for the Deschutes to cut a course among the hard rimrock canyons, but it takes only a day or two to wear a bed into the softer stuff of the soul.

The visual disjunction here—cool, jade water against parched gray stone—is arresting in itself. The conceptual disparity is boggling. That such a river could exist in this dry place, or all this dryness amid such water, seems impossible. To native Westerners, of course, it's just business as usual, and the only strange thing is that the landscape should occasion any comment at all. But coming as I did from the Midwest, where my only trout waters lay hidden in the humid, head-high grasses of dairyland pastures and the jungle-like thickets of northern hardwood forest, a desert trout stream was the ultimate oxymoron, a perfectly irreconcilable internal contradiction. Trout needed water, the desert by definition had none, and that, even I could plainly see, was that.

So when I first saw the Deschutes, the unexpected and overwhelming incongruity of the place jarred me hard enough to cause double vision. One eye rested on the blue ribbon of a thriving trout river; the other on the desiccated, stony hills; and I blinked my brain for days trying to resolve them into a single image that made sense. Measured against what I knew, the landscape registered most powerfully as an absence—no reassuring blanket of topsoil, none of the solace of prolific vegetation, nothing to mitigate the sharp, lunar profile. But subtle places will not be rushed. In later unhurried days and weeks, what inhered in the place gradually came into focus, and I began to recognize that the only sense it made and meaning it had were its own.

The river and its canyon appear to me now a first draft of the world limned in two elemental specifics—the water and the rock—and in them you read an unrevised, original version of all landscape. No expanses of woods or grassland that ripple in the wind, no springy litter of leaves or needles, no movement or resilience to insulate the eye and mind and deceive them into believing the earth itself is something other than stone. The land here concerns rock, water, and bare fact, and these are new truths as well as old ones. The weathered hills, the gorge furrowed deeply into them, the river itself, all seem enduring and ancient, but they are—another incongruity—geologically young. For as long as the river has existed, its course has been formed and reformed dramatically by volcanic activity. Once flowing westward, it was pushed to the north as the volcanoes of the Cascade Range rose high enough to cut off the route to the Pacific. Intermittent activity continued to reshape the watershed as successive lava flows piled layer upon layer over the region. About four million years ago, enormous quantities of molten rock welled up through surface fissures, burying a substantial portion of north-central Oregon in a thick, wrinkled complaint of cooling basalt, through which the Deschutes eventually sculpted a hundred-mile passage to the Columbia River. In the vertical cliffs of dark gray-brown basalt rising from long slopes of scree, you can trace the lamina of this continually recreated landscape, and you're struck, not with how much time it all took but with how little.

The place deceives in other ways. Seeing this arid land as most do, through air conditioning and tinted windows, you can easily mistake the bareness for barrenness. Attuned as we are to the profligacy of forest lands or meadows or coastlines, the high desert seems thin and unpromising. But life has a good hold on the place, wedged among and beneath the stones, in the shade of a sagebrush, up scrub-choked draws, in the cool underground. To observe what lives here, though, takes a keener eye and a more patient patience, and more than any other landscape, this one comes alive most at the edges—at the margins of the day and on the fringe of the river. Deer, antelope, muskrat, mink, otter, skunk, opossum, raccoon, beaver, coyote, all manage a living here. A few are more sinister. Scorpions, though not abundant, hunt in the evening cool. Far more prevalent are the smooth, domed bodies of black widows, glossy as beads of polished coal.

Rattlesnakes, too, are common, though the idea raises its head more frequently than the creature. People who live in rattlesnake country, or even remotely near it, invariably call attention to the fact. It may take the form of a warning, but its real purpose, I think, is to express some elusive, felt quality about the landscape. The mere possibility, however remote, of crossing paths with a rattlesnake imbues the experience of a place with some vital uncertainty or mystery, and so gives it a kind of depth.

Fishermen will treat fish in much the same way. Last summer in Montana, I met an old fisherman on the Madison. He was wading, a little wearily, up the boat ramp at Varney Bridge, and before I could quiz him about his luck, he overflowed with a story about a trout he had released just minutes earlier. A big rainbow, he said, twenty-four inches long, with two scars on its snout. He detailed the particulars about where and how—right over there, he said pointing, on this Royal Wulff right here, and he pointed again. The fish ran over there, and then into that fast water, and he was real lucky to have got that trout, he said, since he was getting to be an old man, and an old man's got old legs, and these old legs, he said, ain't worth a shit.

The following week, and again the week after, I hooked and landed a fish from just the spot he'd pointed out, a fat rainbow with two long parallel scars running slantwise across its nose. Against the scale on my rod, it measured a little over seventeen inches. That it was the same fish I had no doubt. But the old man had still told the truth, or rather, a truth. For him, only a fish that large could begin to bear the weight of the occasion; only a two-foot trout could be commensurate with the emotional size of the event.

The same thing happens with numbers. From time to time I hear stories of deliriously good fishing—days of a hundred trout or more—which, if you pause to figure, comes down to exactly one fish every six minutes of every hour for ten straight hours, without ever stopping to rest, or eat, or answer other calls. I suppose such things happen, but mostly those hundred fish denote a feeling more than a figure. Every yardstick has its own veracity, and the existence of rattlesnakes in a landscape, like pounds or inches or numbers of trout, becomes a kind of shorthand, a fact charged with intense valences tallying some interior significance that goes beyond bare statistics. People talk about bears in just the same way.

Before coming to Oregon, I lived eight years in Virginia and there grew accustomed to the sight of venomous snakes. A friend in the country had a nest of elegantly patterned copperheads somewhere near the house, and one summer his garden teemed with tiny snakelings, coiled on top of cucumber leaves and gliding among the eggplant. (The nest, it turned out, was in his earthen-walled cellar; that autumn, walking down the basement stairs, he was bitten in the foot and spent three days in a hospital.) A lake I used to fish for bass swarmed with water moccasins; rowing the shoreline in a small aluminum jonboat, I'd see a dozen in a day. Once, fishing up Ivy Run, a trickle of water and brook trout in the Blue Ridge Mountains, I came upon an immense Eastern Diamondback, an honest five feet long and as big around as a strong man's forearm. I touched the rattles with my rod tip, and the snake slid lazily off.

I saw a Deschutes rattlesnake on my first trip—a Western Rattler if I read the guidebooks right—and to be honest, was a little disappointed. Still the biggest I've ever run across, the snake measured twenty-four unprepossessing inches, drab, dusty, and unremarkable, built for heat and hard use, and not much interested in living up to my significantly more dramatic expectations. Since then, I've seen a good many more and come to appreciate and admire them. When the fishing is slow, I sometimes poke along the base of canyon walls, watching and listening. They are an abiding Western preoccupation, and simply knowing that you are in "snake country" strops an edge on being there.

That, at any rate, is one response. From time to time, some rural town out here will hold a "rattlesnake roundup," an occasion of great merriment and slaughter where atavistic fears and rattlesnakes are corralled by the crateload under the pretext of good citizenship, handled for sport, milked for the spectacle, killed, eaten, and thoughtfully pronounced to "taste like chicken"—a culinary dubiety ranking second only to something that "isn't too bad when smoked." It does make you wonder, though, what one of those ersatz buckaroos might taste like to a snake.

What lives here mirrors the landscape itself—hard, thorny or spined, leathery, chitinous or scaled. But for all the apparent durability and resistance, it is a delicate world, establishing itself with difficulty, growing slowly, and uncertain to rebound if disturbed. Evidence of this abounds as the usual lineup of suspects—intensive monoculture farming, irrigation, grazing, well-intentioned fire-fighting, and relentless recreational use—have all humbled the landscape, of which more, inevitably.

The river has a better grip, and if this too is only seeming, it's at least more convincing. Some years ago, the ordinarily equivocal hand of resource management was laid upon the river, or more precisely upon the fishery (it has yet to extend significantly to the river itself). In this instance, the fate proved a happy one. Barbless hooks became a requirement, fishing from boats was prohibited, minimum stream flows were guaranteed, stocking curtailed, and anachronistically generous bag limits restricted. The current slot limit, two fish between ten and thirteen inches, has made the river a *de facto* no-kill area, since almost no one bothers to keep so few smallish trout. As a result, the fishing in the Deschutes is better now than it has been for decades, and you can call it progress, even if the trajectory is not forward but backward to an earlier age of abundance.

Rivers are remarkable things this way. Provided they haven't been dammed out of existence (a large provision these days), they resuscitate themselves at the slightest provocation, especially when compared to the slow recovery of terrestrial landscapes. Biologically, the case is pretty straightforward. Short-lived, quickly maturing species, like most fish, aquatic insects, and vegetation, have short reproductive cycles and tend to be prolific propagators. When some external threat—overfishing, erosion, drawdown, or pollution—is eliminated, life rushes back to refill the river. Then, too, the simple fact of moving water accelerates the process, flushing the river free of all sorts of garbage and helping to distribute rapidly the organisms that populate and repopulate the stream. Even when given the chance, white rhinos and California redwoods require far longer convalescence.

Beyond this, rivers fare better than the land for the simple fact that most of them are never owned. The way they can, gradually or quickly, shrink or overflow or change course defies the notion of boundaries and renders rivers uncomfortably difficult to see as property. The surveyor's stakes that mince a landscape into real estate are nearly as hard to drive into a stream as into the air. The land is emphatically there; a river is just passing through, the paradox of permanent transience that must unsettle those who bank on the apparent fixity of possession. A landowner has the dispensation of his ownership to do pretty much as he pleases with the land, but rivers can't be bought and sold, which makes them something of an American anomaly and preserves them, to a degree, from the general afflictions of private custody. If this seems cynical, consider that the enormities perpetrated upon many a river have come precisely at the hands of those who think that they own it, or more to the point, act like they do.

The Deschutes has suffered its share of this sort of thing, but has adjusted, accommodated the modern world, and, under somewhat diminished circumstances, flourished. Cool water still slides below rocky cliffs. Beneath the currents are the stones and under the stones, at the bottom of it all, are the stoneflies.

In the universe of trout waters, some places are defined by the fish or the fishing; I think of the Bow, the Green, the Bighorn, the San Juan. On others, the Beaverkill, the Campbell, the North Umpqua, the fishing is inseparable from a fertile tradition and history. A small handful of waters, though, find their conceptual centers in a bug and become synonymous with a hatch: the Green Drake on Henrys Fork, the sulfury *dorothea* on the Letort, the *Hexagenia* of Michigan's Au Sable. And on the Deschutes, the giant black stonefly, *Pteronarcys californica*. Perhaps owing to the long-standing enmity between Oregonians and the Mongol hordes of California, the insects are never referred to by the species designation, but are simply called "salmonflies." It fits well enough. Between the abdominal segments and at the articulation points of the legs, the body coloration changes from smoky gray to a pinkish-orange almost precisely the shade of salmon flesh. Though the actual amount of the body tinted this shade is small, it calls a disproportionate attention to itself, and the overall impression of the insect in flight is a whirr of a pale burnt-orange.

There are other good hatches on the Deschutes, more prolific emergences and possibly even better fishing, but the stonefly hatch eclipses all others and with good reason. By trout-stream standards, the insect is gargantuan. A mature nymph may be as big as a man's little finger, and although the body of the adult is bit smaller, the long, veined wings make it appear even larger than the nymph. I recall reading once that according to an aerodynamic analysis of wing area and beat frequency, body weight and wind resistance, a bumblebee shouldn't be able to fly. The same calculations would probably be at an equal loss to explain why stoneflies fly so badly. Despite four sizable and powerful-looking wings, they labor through the air, abdomen and legs drooping down, head leaning forward, not so much flying as lunging from place to place. For this, or some other reason, the winged adults, like the nymphs, wisely prefer to crawl, shunning the light and keeping to the underside of things.

Apart from their obvious appeal to fish, big flies themselves hold a particular fascination for fishermen, and I'm drawn to such hatches as much for the flies as the fishing. Even on large rivers, most insects are small, and most of what they do is obscured by the scale on which it takes place. Even close up, a mayfly hatches unobtrusively; from a little farther away the event is all but invisible. You can see the hatch generally and collectively, but only rarely the individual episodes that constitute it. The whole affair is engineered precisely not to call attention to itself, and getting a clear, close look takes an effort significantly out of proportion to the size of the object. The capture of an airborne mayfly dun, out of pure curiosity or the hatch-matcher's business, makes up in difficulty what it lacks in dignity. Determined anglers in boots of clay, with fly rods held protectively in attitudes of graceful extension, leap feeble little leaps and scoop clumsily at empty air, like a pod of hippos gravely dancing *Swan Lake*. Strictly speaking, you often don't see the hatch at all; you infer it from riseforms, fish behavior, and all the usual clues. Under ordinary circumstances, a trout stream is an inconspicuous world, though the fish of course manage just fine.

Good-sized flies, though, amplify what surrounds them, scaling the whole scene nearer the reach of human perception and giving you a sense, for a little while, of what it would be like to have really good eyes. When the light is right, I can watch a stonefly twirling and drifting in eddies fifty yards away on the far side of the Deschutes. The riseforms of trout, often surprisingly subtle in this swift water, are magnified as well. The big flies trigger startling, explosive rises from larger fish, while gangs of four-inch trout will snap at a waterborne adult and churn the water as they hound it downriver, trying to choke down a meal as big as a half-smoked cigar.

The size of the stonefly, too, becomes something of a compensation, since the emergence itself lacks a little in drama. A mayfly or caddis hatch comes off with a sense of style and flair; the nymphs rise from the riverbed, float upward, and burst into wing on the surface in a grandly overcomplicated spectacle. But a stonefly nymph does not suddenly levitate into adulthood. It walks, plodding resolutely shoreward, usually at night, and creeping up the bank, takes its time squirming out of the nymphal case—a far more prosaic affair than a good mayfly hatch, but also proof that nature does not invariably do things the hard way. Should you leave a fly rod propped overnight against a streamside tree or a pair of wading boots at the water's edge, by morning they'll be spattered with husky nymphal shucks that crumble to the touch like last year's leaves. The bankside grasses and trees will have a fresh coat of new stoneflies, scuttering about, amicably sharing mates, and falling into the water just often enough to keep the trout alert and well fed.

This kind of activity naturally garners a good bit of attention. The fish slip in from deeper water to take up stations closer to the bank and nearer the likelihood of good dining. Swallows careen above the river with their peculiar creaking call, like the groan of a rocking chair or an old oak floor. At night, great numbers of bats take their place.

The hatch has drawn me here too, along with the rest of the world, or at least the ever-expanding part of it that fishes. And they are finally the reason I'm deeply ambivalent about returning each year.

It is a constant temptation, as constantly indulged, to carp about the number of other fishermen around these days, particularly among those who took up fly fishing long before it ceased to be a sport and became a growth industry. The Deschutes has not yet reached the unconstrained Malthusian insanity of major tailwaters like the Green or Bighorn, though it may be only a matter of time before the number of stonefly fishermen and the number of stoneflies are dead even. Yuppies characteristically take much of the heat for this, and they are an easy and understandably gratifying target. But I suspect that the mass intrusion into fly fishing of these annoyingly be-Volvoed apparitions, with impeccable gear and perfect teeth, is pretty much figmentary. My truck mechanic, the UPS driver, the guy who installed my furnace, all recent fly fishermen, inhabit the middle world where pinpointing villains verges perilously on self-incrimination. Of the phenomenon itself, the crowding and overcrowding of streams, there can be no doubt. But the fishing world is full of people, and everybody is one of them and becomes, from time to time, a piece of someone else's problem and an occasion for their resentment.

The much-insinuated moral superiority of fly fishing, and (happy coincidence) of fly fishermen, is precisely the cheese that it appears. But I will say this: A fly-fishing crowd rarely turns ugly, and dubious as that is as a claim to virtue, in this part of the country it does stand for something. The bigger salmon and steelhead rivers here draw bait and hardware fishermen shoulder-to-shoulder in outrageous numbers, and they can get a little testy. Sarcasm is routine, harsh words not uncommon, and I've heard more than one reliable account of sidearms waved vaguely around, though none of actual shots being fired. The best holes on some rivers are cordoned off by strings of linked boats that are accurately, if obliviously, termed by the participants themselves, "hoglines," and any innocent intruder or unsanctioned hog-aspirant is dealt with severely. About all you can do is cut a wide swath around such large-scale malfunctions and take some solace in the fact that the most fitting retribution is to leave them in the company of one another. "Abu garcia," says my wife, "may his tribe decrease."

This kind of behavior crops up far less among fly fishermen if only for logistical reasons. The sweep of a backcast and forecast effectively stakes out a piece of the river. Another fisherman who infringes upon that territory is likely to find a fly line hissing past his ear regularly enough to make the encroachment more trouble than it's worth. Flyfishing custom, too, dictates even larger cushions of space between anglers, and for the most part they remain out of convenient insult range and beyond the reach of all but practiced marksmen.

Even so, personal space is a circumstantial and negotiable commodity; that a fly fisherman requires more of it merely means that a river fills up faster. Turf wars ensue, though they are tactical rather than combative, waged silently in a complex system of snubs, preemptive positionings, and discreet gestures charged with meaning. Every angler radiates a force field, a little zone of sovereignty he carries with him up and down the river, shrinking or enlarging it according to the character and promise of the water he's fishing. The slightest trespass on the farthest limits reverberates faithfully to the center, like a moving magnet inducing current in an electrical wire.

The Deschutes itself contributes to the problem. As trout rivers go, it is a big one, and though theoretically this should mitigate crowding by allowing anglers to spread out, in reality just the opposite happens. Much of the water is swift and deep right up to the edge of its brushy banks, and, for all practical purposes, unwadable. The river is as yet too young to have worn itself into the more approachable pool-and-riffle configuration of a mature watercourse, so a large number of fishermen are funnelled into comparatively few spots and predictable consequences.

My favorite stonefly section of the river flows around an island just large enough to have created a slow, wide flat, perhaps a hundred yards long, below it. The easy wading makes this stretch popular, and I hiked up to it a few seasons ago little expecting to find any room. It was already eight A.M. At peak season, the hardcores arrive before dawn to scour the place with big black nymphs. Nine fishermen—three too many under the best of circumstances—had already taken up positions when I got there. I sat down at the tail of the run to watch.

For as long as I'd been fishing the flat, a pair of Canada geese had nested on the downstream tip of the island. The point offered all the amenities: good protection, an unobstructed view of all likely approaches to the nest, a plot of tender grass, and immediate access to shallow water with an abundance of aquatic vegetation. It was prime real estate, and this year a second pair of geese had apparently bid for a hostile takeover. All four of the birds were intensely occupied in a dispute that consisted mainly of meticulously struck, stylized poses. The slightly elevated wings quivered in warning. The head bent low to the ground might be mistaken for a gesture of submission if it weren't for the arched neck, reproducing precisely the shape of that final curve behind the head of a coiled rattlesnake, cocked like a firing pin. (Even ignoring the fact that a goose can bite like a sonofabitch, it can deliver a pretty solid wallop with its wing and isn't a quarter the coward a rattlesnake is. All else being equal, I'd rather run into the snake.) Each goose assumed the same posture, a slight movement on the part of one answered with countermovement from the others, always resolving back to static tension and scrupulously maintained distances. Then without warning, responding to the kind of cues whose meaning is apparent only to the species in question, whether they be geese or baboons or fly fishermen, the intruding pair simply straightened up, turned around, and swam away.

They swam, in fact, within a close cast of the first fisherman below the island, who responded by sidestepping downstream and out farther into the river, tipping the balance so that the angler below him shuffled downriver a few rod lengths, encroaching on the water of the next man down, who adjusted his position, and so on down to the ninth man who, already fishing marginal water, waded out in a splashy huff and left. I slipped in and took his place. Having not yet fished that morning, I was impatient to have at it, and must have projected a particularly militant sense of personal fishing space, because it bumped my upstream neighbor up farther still, and over the next half-hour, the remaining seven fishermen in turn all jostled and adjusted until the last exasperated angler was pushed almost to the point of the island, and equilibrium was regained. The defeated pair of geese, already smarting from territorial imperatives, felt the squeeze from both sides and took off.

I probably should have just done the same, of course, but with eight fishermen above me, I nonetheless tilled my little plot of water with the exaggerated deliberateness of a man nursing his last cigarette, dividing the currents into subcurrents, then microcurrents, putting ten minutely spaced casts where I'd normally put one, close-reading the text of the water with the hyperanalytical exhaustiveness of an untenured English professor, and to roughly the same end.

This kind of fishing is a fatiguing act of imagination, and when it became clear that the eight people upstream had given up fishing for homesteading, I waded out, scrambled up the steep bank, and headed upstream for my ace-in-the-hole, a spot of last resort because of its technical difficulties. Out in the middle, the river shallows to less than a foot in depth, and between the shoal and the left hand bank runs a moderately deep channel perhaps sixty yards long. For much of its length, overhanging alders droop nearly to the surface; beneath them, big trout wait in shade and patience. I tucked a box of flies and some tippet material in a shirt pocket and took off my vest. To get a functional casting position here, you must crouch in the current nearly to your wadertops, and, with rod parallel to the water's surface and only inches above it, reach out over the river and shoot angling casts back to the bank underneath the trees. One in four might hit the mark. In high-water years, the arching limbs skim the river, and fishing is out of the question. Once a spot has been worked, you inch a course over a riverbed of wobbly, angular boulders until you find the footing for another series of casts. It can take two hours to work the entire run, most of it spent not fishing.

On the first two casts to make the water, a pair of seven-inch steelhead smolts pestered a Goddard caddis until they hooked themselves. Schools of these fish, along with salmon smolt, flock to the bankside eddies, and they're easily distinguished from the resident rainbows by their silvery color and sleek, bullet-shaped forms. They're surprisingly strong for their size, and some days you catch one after another after another. But their pecking hits left me completely unprepared for the deep boil beneath the fly a few casts later. Seconds elapsed before I could gather myself, and I struck with a pointless, full-body convulsion that buried thirty feet of fly line and leader high in the alders behind me.

The chance to fish dry flies to these big Deschutes rainbows, locally called "redsides" for the obvious reason, is the great promise of the stonefly hatch. But much as I court the opportunity, it always unnerves me. Yanking the fly line free, I frantically gnawed off the broken tippet and knotted on a huge adult stonefly pattern, an explosion of elk hair and hackle bearing striking resemblance to a small gerbil that has just chewed its way through a toaster cord. The fish concurred, and some minutes later I tiptoed on.

It was midday by now, and as usual a stiff wind had kicked up, shaking the alders and depositing an occasional stonefly on the surface. Two long casts above me, I heard the implosive snap of a rise and looked up in time to see a slow, swirling vortex of the kind made only by a large fish, whose most leisurely movements displace an impressive quantity of water. I marked the spot and continued working toward it, wanting to fish the run properly, with care and ripening expectation.

A second sound followed almost immediately, the unmistakable metallic grind of aluminum on cobbles. An obviously new Alumaweld driftboat, a high-sided guide's model emblazoned with the three-color logo of a fly shop, had dropped anchor on the shoal, and a pair of bulky neoprened wursts struggled over the gunnel. The guide stood and pointed, and the two sports shuffled their way nearer to the achingly fine little chute where I'd marked the trout. The fish hit on the second cast. On the trip downriver, it passed within a rod-length of me, and not long after, the guide waded to the tail of the shoal thirty feet below the fisherman and netted a thick rainbow that went a year or two past twenty inches.

A few more casts and they were back in the boat, cutting a wide path around me in ostentatious deference to my fishing, as though somehow they hadn't carved the tenderloin from my water, and screwed me. I might have bulled my way up the bank when they first arrived and shot a seventy-foot prayer up to the trout, but in having been forced to fish by their rules, I would have been screwed anyway. Drifting past, the lucky sport flashed me an ambiguous thumbs-up sign as I receded in the distance, watching with the dazed ineffectuality of a sitcom husband. I patted my pockets—fresh out of lithium gum—and, too late, I raised a digit of my own.

These little competitions can suck you into escalating cycles before you realize it. They become oddly personal, and, somewhere along the way, the fishing slips into covetousness and resentment. Wading fishermen are bad enough. Boaters complicate the picture, particularly the rafters, staggering numbers of whom descend the river in what is unsympathetically known as "the rubber hatch." Some of these people fish, and relations with the wading angler are chilly. Poised high on thrones of hypalon and aluminum, they drift through your water with a blank, aristocratic indifference. They've been casting since dawn, covered miles of river and will fish miles more, and disturbing one little fishing spot is a trifling affair, particularly if it is yours. They stare as they pass, regarding with godlike contempt the pitiful labor of your wading, the limited scope of your water, the littleness of your thinking.

Most of the rafters, however, come for the whitewater downriver, and if their use is recreational, their mere presence at times seems a species of vandalism. Oversized tape players boom the outdoor-enhancing stuff of heavy metal and rap, over which they scream to be heard. Beery frat boys straddle the tubes of giant Rikens and carom through the Class IV water at Whitehorse and Boxcar. Every few years, the cops fish a carcass from the river somewhere near Maupin or below Sherars Falls, though fortunately this appears to have no ill effect on the fishing.

Today, the rafters drifted quietly by as, to be fair, they often do. But last night, one of the big guided parties beached at the campground with all the self-possession of Cortez among the Aztecs. There are only a few areas on the river open to camping, and these are often full to choking, a fact lost on no one, though all attempts at an administrative Heimlich maneuver have so far failed. By ten this morning, there was only the stunning aftermath of their garbage.

All this commotion has been enough to piss off the Indians who live on the Warm Springs Reservation and own thirty miles of the river's far bank. History is nothing if not symmetrical, and the dynamics of past centuries are mirrored in this one. The disputes among sheep herders, cattle ranchers, and Indians have been recast among fishermen, rafters, and the much-diminished pockets of Native Americans. These altercations used to be called "range wars"; now they are termed "user conflicts," but their occasions—land, water, resources—remain as unchanged as their goal, which in the end is power. The dissonances of the landscape find a garbled echo in human discord, and the river and its canyon enclose a complete history of the West. The railroads even fought it out here once.

There was never really any Warm Springs tribe, though there is now. In 1855, with one gun trained on the Indians and another pointed squarely at its own foot, the government rounded up scattered bands—Paiutes; the Wyam, Tenino, Dock-spus, and Taih of the Walla Wallas; the Ki-Gal-Twal-La and Dog River bands of the Wascos; and others—starving them first for enhanced cooperation, and deposited them on 137,000 acres of inconsequence that bordered the Deschutes on the east. Now, largely by historical accident, the Confederated Tribes of Warm Springs have become a factor in the river's fate and a force to be reckoned with, though like most of us, they have devolved into political category, mere containers for the "Native American perspective" that must be "taken into account" before it is ignored. Well-intentioned as some of this has been, the drop from "cause" to "commodity" is a short sure one here in McAmerica, where tying a bit of colored ribbon around an automobile antenna is regarded as serious political involvement. The Indians have become the object of social ambulance-chasers and New Age spiritual hitchhikers whose attentions, however innocent, reduce to a form of cultural gawking.

Which is all to say that it's not surprising the Indians get a bit perturbed at times, though despite this, you can buy a two-dollar day-pass to fish the reservation. I suppose the tribal authorities will eventually realize that so many miles of prime frontage on blue-ribbon trout and steelhead water is in fact a small gold mine. That, and the prospect of yanking the white man around a little may prove unendurably tempting, and things will change. For now, their tolerance is a form of subsidy, spreading the fishermen out and in a modest way mitigating the crowding problem.

The obvious solution to all of this is just to leave and go home, wedge my Deschutes fishing into cracks and crannies of the year, and nibble at the edge of its seasons, though this has the disturbing feel of letting someone else lead your life. Or fish somewhere else, maybe saltwater, where a few frustrated trout fishermen have found a frontiersman's refuge, working the surf or cruising bluewater for billfish and shark, though I've never much cared for this kind of parlor stunt, nor shown much aptitude for it.

But I can't seem to leave this place—its big flies and big fish and its immense, contradictory beauties. Sometimes the brain has a mind of its own, and the paradox inhering in the landscape is as well a free-floating thing that imbues our experience of the place. It takes shape in me as a deep ambivalence, and I present to myself the ridiculous spectacle of something pinned by one wing, fluttering madly and flapping itself senseless against the stones. Many of the regulars feel like this, having fished the year round, through bad weather and lean seasons. The stonefly hatch comes as a kind of harvest, something they've earned and are entitled to, and the crowds that follow seem a variety of locust descending to feed on fat times.

All of this, I hope, is not as monumentally ungenerous as it must appear, to complain about those who only do as I do and want what I want. I could as easily figure as an unwelcome character in someone else's peevish little narrative. I'm certain I have. And in a way, this is precisely the point and for me the most unsettling paradox of fishing stoneflies in this stony country: a circumstance that should encourage and enlarge the best impulses of the spirit—the office, I think, of any authentic passion—can instead foster some of the worst. It isn't the people I resent, or their sport I begrudge, but the inability to incorporate them into my universe of trout fishing.

The momentum of a passion drives in many directions, and to me fly fishing, at its best (which it usually is), can take you outside of yourself, which means a good deal more than simply leaving behind the worries and irritations of daily existence. The effect is less "away" than "apart," a space where, with a little humility, I am convinced, I might be able to learn something.

Under other circumstances, like sharing home water with a couple hundred other unshaven lunatics, the momentum travels differently, pushing inward toward and upon yourself. I learn something here too. We are our extravagances. In just the measure we invest in them, they show us to ourselves, and self-discovery is apt to be a brutally indiscriminate thing. I begin to suspect I am an asshole.

As more and more fishermen arrive, and more driftboats slap and rattle their way through the chop, the entire stonefly phenomenon seems destined for critical mass. But at times fly fishermen, like children, inhabit a state of grace, and rather than culminating in some heated chain reaction, the spectacle decays into exactly the kind of daily circus that most people came here to escape. Paradoxically, this is its saving power—pressed to its limits, the whole scene reveals itself as essentially comic. By any measure, the stakes are tiny except for the few testosterone-fueled enigmas and their take-no-prisoners fishing, casting and racking up the score to prove something to or about themselves. And if these are not fundamentally comic, they are at least comical.

In quantum physics, subatomic particles are assigned a number "S," which designates a property known as "strangeness." Physicists have always been keen on saving things, and in nuclear reactions, as there is a conservation of energy and conservation of momentum, so there is a conservation of strangeness, which goes to show that modern science makes more sense of the world than is commonly supposed.

Big things mirror small ones, and there comes a point when the accrued strangeness transforms the Deschutes from crowded trout stream to a bizarre species of theme park: Six Thousand Rods Over Oregon. Along the best runs, anglers line up patiently to take three-for-a-quarter casts at stuffed trout. Parades of RV battlecruisers rumble into the campground and unfurl broad mats of astroturf and little American flags. Ropey men with tattoos and bad teeth lug bales of hay. Immense striped awnings sprout like mushrooms; guylines, tent ropes, and strings of Japanese lanterns spread like mycelia across the desert dust. Along the banks, inner tubes and Day-Glo plastic rafts wait to buoy the spawn of a thousand campers. Somewhere, a band strikes up, and in huddled en-claves, there is talk of electing a Stonefly Queen.

When evening falls at last, the sounds of radios and boozy laughter rise above the collective white-noise hiss of countless Coleman lanterns. Picking my way carefully through the glare, I hike up to the cool lip of the rimrock canyon, and, with a 6-cell Maglite, vainly signal the mother ship to pick me up.

8

Thy Rod
and Thy Radish

The man pulling radishes

pointed my way

with a radish.

—Issa

Someone once asked Ray Charles what the worst part of being blind was; he replied, "Not being able to see." Some things are pointedly obvious, and for that reason alone are easily overlooked.

Trout streams, too, are obvious in their way, and looking without overlooking asks for a special kind of sight.

If you spend much time at all outdoors, you soon discover a peculiar thing about vision: Sometimes the best way to see something is by *not* looking directly at it. On a moonless night, observe a star, not Sirius or Vega or any of the first-magnitude bodies, but one of the thousands of second- or third-magnitude stars. Before long, the light begins to undulate and flicker. Squint to quiet the image into definition, and it grows more inconstant still. Stare hard enough, and the star swims into the black-hole blind spot of your eye and vanishes altogether. But if you observe the image askance and focus on the empty space to one side, the star returns and resolves into fixity, settling not at the center of sight but a few degrees away on the periphery.

Naturalists, bird-watchers, and hunters come to learn much the same thing. Movement often registers most readily on the outskirts of the visual field, and they will slowly scan a landscape less to locate a specific object than to shift the compass of peripheral apprehension. An elk lifting its head to listen, a wild turkey scratching for mast, the staccato twitch of a gray squirrel's tail—these are best caught in the corner of your eye where you see with an unwatchful attention.

But this kind of vision that observes apparently nothing to perceive something requires practice. Habit tempts the brain and eye to inch their way back and center the image, vaguely uneasy with the parallax of uncoupling the line of direct vision from that of direct awareness. The mind sees as the eye does and can obscure a thing by staring too intently, blinding itself with the effort of its own discernment. The path of most sensitive perception is often indirect.

A friend of mine teaches printmaking and drawing. As a simple exercise in vision, he asks his students to sketch from a landscape photograph he is holding. He allows them to study the picture briefly, but a moment before the students begin drawing, he turns the photograph upside-down, jarring them from recognized details to an obliquity of essential shapes, contrasts, and relations. They no longer have trees and hills and so can no longer reproduce in pencil any familiar ideas about these things. Without the framework of already-understood objects, they must see the subject by not seeing it.

It is the same, I think, with rivers. They too are best approached obliquely, approached as Barry Lopez says of deserts (which are far less antithetical to rivers than might be supposed) "with no intentions of discovery." A river, like the aurora borealis or a landscape or a radish, is only itself and has no way to resist being channeled into preconceptions or

filtered through assumptions that falsify what it is. Come upon a river
with purpose, or desire, or ideas, or even words and you merely make it
into these things. We have overlooked countless rivers by seeing them
just this way—that is, by not really seeing them at all.

So I've always found it best to come in on a tangent, asymptotically,
crabwise. And it helps to bring good optics. The occupation of discovering a river begins with preoccupation, some focal point that deflects
awareness away from the subject and so sensitizes the periphery. For me,
fly fishing offers just this type of lens. For others, it may be dabbing at a
tray of watercolors, taking an aimless walk, or playing the cello. Anything
will do as long as it suspends the mind's propensity to replicate itself in
whatever it dwells on, and leaves clear the edges of acumen to be im-
pinged upon, sidelong and incidentally, by what is really there. Only then
do you begin to know what to look for and get some idea of how it may
be found.

Even the most tamed and domesticated river is still a wild thing and,
like all wild things, must be waited out. Then one day you suddenly look
up and a hundred happenstances are unexpectedly startled into sense.
The object is not to ambush the river, to catch it unaware and surprise it
into showing itself. The idea is to trick yourself out of yourself, where
you can get a better look.

The approach is not without obstacles. Nature survives by misdirection, by feints and sleight-of-hand. The patterned skin of a rattlesnake
twisting through weeds momentarily baffles the eye, which cannot determine what direction the snake is headed or whether it's moving at all.
The flashing eyespots on butterfly wings, half-glimpsed through the
grass, look strangely like something else. Possums do indeed play possum.

Rivers also show a direction that is as well a misdirection. Taking
our cues from the current, we regard their trajectory always downstream,
and so look at them in reverse. Though they flow forward, rivers reach
back, branching and rebranching between ridges, into the folds of hills,
up to the tiniest valleys, back into crevices and creases, spreading at last
between the grains of soil. Every square millimeter of earth is a watershed, and a river the most comprehensive expression of a landscape. That
it resembles in this way the architecture of circulation, of arteries, and

venules, and capillaries is more than coincidence. Rivers transfuse the land and pump it full of life, our ordinary vocabulary of "drainages" notwithstanding.

Such misdirections—the camouflaging vermiculations on a brook trout's back, the detached and wiggling tail of a gecko—may be ambivalent, preserving the prey while depriving the predator, but they are quite literally true to nature. Words, however, are another matter and insofar as they give shape to what we see, a more serious one. Despite what you may read, rivers can't "sing" and they don't "dance"; they can't "chatter merrily" or "rush with impatience"; pools don't "brood" and riffles don't "laugh." As many fishermen know, and many writers seem not to, people do these things; trout streams cannot. A river dances only in print, the author's trained monkey whose performance is unwitting and meaningless.

The problem with dancing rivers and the like is not so much that the visual evocations are often ludicrous, but that they are false. Such images represent less a failure of imagination than of sensibility. Perceiving a river in human terms preempts what it may actually be. This kind of anthropomorphism is as old as storytelling itself and perhaps once served the purpose of taming an often terrifying and foreign wilderness by humanizing it. A volcano could still destroy, but to conceive of the mountain as "angry" at least made the behavior knowable and familiar, and so less threatening, because we saw it as a version of ourselves. Such fears have become largely irrelevant in the modern world. What was once the chief condition of existence—men living at the dangerous and unpredictable whims of nature—has gradually given way to its opposite, and investing the natural world with human behaviors has become suspect. The whole enterprise attempts to make something more out something already whole—and ends up making it less.

A dancing river involves as well its measure of arrogance. I read recently, in an otherwise thoughtful and careful book, a passage in which the author describes catching his first trout of the new season: "two tugs . . . the second as a trout takes hold with what can only be described as a hearty handshake of welcome." It's safe to say that "welcome" was the last thing on this trout's mind, and making the acquaintance of the

writer an experience it would just as soon forgo. This fisherman is warm-
ly greeting his own metaphor, heartily shaking hands with himself. The
literature of angling (and outdoor sport in general) routinely trades in
such clean, well-lighted fatuities, narcissistically recasting the natural
world in the writer's own image. He doesn't see what a trout does; he
sees only how he thinks he would behave if he were a fish. This habit of
mind deals with the things of nature as though they are people, and, giv-
en human history, this is a pretty shabby way to treat them.

And even when the terms aren't human—big fish called "hogs," or
"gators," or "toads"—they seem to proceed from the assumption that fish
and fishing must be made into something else before they can be appreciated. The results are an unpalatable disfigurement of some original
essence, like a piece of airline chicken.

Naturally it's a matter of taste and perspective, but perspective, the
angle of vision, is precisely what's at stake here. In some points of view,
"getting back to nature" means buying up every square foot of real estate
you can lay your hands on and bulldozing it into a golf course. To make a
river dance is finally an act of domination, the verbal analog of clearcuts
and dams, and if this seems farfetched, consider that all resource-based
industries embody and justify their perspectives in the words they use:
"harvest," "management," "multiple use," "yield," "salvage," "production goals," "surplus," and the very term "resource" itself. It is far less disturbing to employ the vocabularies of commerce and agriculture than to
speak the language of individual rivers, stands of old growth, or ecosys-
tems. Words can mold our vision to see one thing as another, making it
less troublesome and more susceptible to control, and in the end elimi-
nating any reason to see it differently. In *Upland Stream*, W. D. Wetherell,
writing of his home water, Copper Run in New Hampshire, articulates
the cycle: "For the devaluation of words makes for a devaluation of the
things words describe, and sets up a vicious circle from which there is no
escape. With fewer words left to describe our Copper Runs, it becomes
harder to justify saving them; as the Copper Runs vanish, the need for a
language to describe them vanishes as well."

This is not just the stuff of logging companies and the Army Corps
of Engineers. Fishing writers are implicated as well, though with less ob-

viously dramatic consequences. Catching fish is often envisioned, and so described, as a "contest," a "battle," "a matching of wits," "a competition," some "game" we play with the trout. They paint a picture in which equal opponents square off in a friendly and fair fight, and may the best man win. Congenial as they make the experience, such images are enormously deceptive. Fish, I think we can reasonably assume, do not enjoy being caught. To them, fishing is not a "game" or a "dance," and although a hook may quite possibly cause them no pain, anyone who fishes can see that being hooked alarms the hell out of them. To write as though it were somehow otherwise obscures the ethical dimension of what we do, a dimension that many fly fishermen are willing to confront only to a point. Catch-and-release may be good conservation, but it is ethically ambiguous. Between the man who kills and eats a fish and the man who derives pleasure from a trout's panicked struggles, it's worth asking who occupies the moral high ground. Or if there is any.

Gutting an antelope, bloody to his elbows and reaching for viscera deep within the body cavity, Tom McGuane tells of his sudden awareness that "This is goddamned serious." Precisely the same holds for fishing, even if there are fewer guts, or none at all. Stripped of the opaqueness of euphemism, a central truth of fishing emerges—nothing, not fish, not fisherman, just lives; they all live at the expense of something else. On a purely biological level, we must kill to survive. On an psychic one, we kill to survive as well. Human weakness is undeniably strong and quite possibly inevitable. It may even be necessary. We choose our battles, and to continue living at all requires certain insensitivities. Ritualizing them doesn't change the fact, though ritual may help to forgive it.

I fish as often as I can, invariably with great pleasure, and frankly I don't often give these things much thought. But when I do, they are the reason fishing makes sense, what makes fishing a serious business and separates it from something like golf, which will always be simply a sport because at the core it has no meaning. Fishing is not apart from life, nor like life, and is no more a "metaphor" for life than a pregnant woman is. It is the thing itself.

I used to keep fishing records obsessively—a stage, I think, that every serious angler enters into and sometimes passes out of—and compiled detailed logs of weather information, river levels, fish activity, hatches, successful patterns and failed ones, moon phases, and all the rest, including interesting birds or animals I'd seen or curiosities encountered. Before a trip, I'd consult these logs, take notes on the notes, and as result I found myself more often at approximately the right place, with nearly the right flies, at the more or less right time. I made no quantum leaps in skill or knowledge, but gained little by little in both.

Ironically, the most precise event these records show is the day they stopped—June 11, 1987—and since then the entries have dwindled to sketchy, *pro forma* business documentations, nuisances perpetrated at the behest of others. The date holds no particular significance that I can recall. At some point around that time, I must simply have become aware that the observations I'd logged were no more "fishing" than a map of a place is the place itself. My records were both accurate and distorted, a Mercator projection of experience that pictured in two dimensions what really existed in three and made the catching of fish as big as Greenland. It occurred to me one day that I was standing in my own way.

As habits of vision, "looking" and "looking for" seem to me very different routes to pursue. The former has a goal, the latter an endpoint, and the difference between them is the difference between knowing a thing and simply knowing about it. This is scarcely a novel idea; it has only the newness of individual rediscovery. Your Zen types are fond of saying that "the goal is the path"—an apparently muddled conflation of ends and means until you recognize that a path is not always or necessarily a path *to* somewhere. Or rather, it isn't a path to anywhere other than where it happens to be at the moment. The goal is the place itself, or the succession of places along the way—not as destinations, but as promontories or prospects. The meaning is in the perspective and the framing of simple particularities that are only themselves. From the absurdly wonderful intricacies of a hatching mayfly, to a muddy radish, how you see is what you see.

By luck or intention, fly fishing has built into itself this same idea. In what is to me one of angling's most elegant expressions, we speak of "reading the water." Reading a trout stream exercises a special kind of vision and, like reading anything, acknowledges that meaning dwells in contexts and on peripheries and that not all things come to the eye with equal readiness. So you take up a vantage point and cast a fly or paint a picture or bow a cello, and wait yourself out. From the edges, the river converges into focus; the boundary between occupation and preoccupation dissolves; the difference between seeing the river and fishing it or painting it or walking along its banks becomes a trifling matter of emphasis.

If you can forget what others have said or written, and resist their efforts to transform a river into something else, the river will transform you. A friend with whom I sometimes fish, a freelance journalist with the aptly piscatorial name, Adelheid Fischer, once wrote that one of the most remarkable things about a trout stream is "the person I become when I'm near one." This seems to me exactly right, though a far cry from the bogus feel-goodism purveyed in the inanities of psycho-pop and situation comedies. It is a quality of feeling earned by a quality of vision, one that "sees things steadily and sees them whole." I don't think I'm stretching the matter at all to say that given half a chance, a trout stream can make you a better person.

This isn't particularly a reason that I fish, but certainly one of things I like about it.

Just fishing won't do, of course. Fishing can be as much an act of domination as building a dam or turning Yellowstone into a thousand-unit condo with heated pools and a waterslide for the kids. In some hands, a river merely becomes a gigantic canvas on which to paint deeply unattractive self-portraits. A friend of mine calls such people "fishing jocks," for whom trout cease to be simply challenging; they become "a challenge" and catching them becomes just another species of touch-down pass. But a river is only itself. If forced, the water will mirror the likeness of an ego; on its own, it reflects only sky and clouds, and readily rewards those who approach it with humility and wonder.

Still, we see some rivers better than we see others. For whatever reason—our histories with them, an unusually powerful aesthetic rapport, some unspecifiable eloquence—a few such rivers, perhaps only one, come into focus for each of us more readily and significantly than the rest. They grow into places of deep fixity in life and align themselves like compass points in the mind's geography. My own such water is a fine, clear, spring creek, small by most measures, but substantial enough in its way to furnish just this kind of anchor for the spirit. When times come, as they invariably do, when what is needed most is a form of existential triage, I am certain that if I can just get back to this place, equilibrium will somehow return. If the word "balm" describes anything, it is this water. I don't know whether this means that my stream is a starting point or an ending point. Perhaps just a point of vantage. But I think that this feeling, more than anything, is what is meant when fishermen speak of "home water." Such places manage to draw from us the best qualities of something like a soul and put them within reach.

This is quite likely true of any passion but may be especially so of fishing, because the irreducible constant of fishing is water. We may, as some university biologists have argued, harbor a buried affinity for open grasslands, the remnant of some racial memory of our savannah-wandering ancestors. But water is a more ancient and elemental kind of genetic beacon. Though named for a whale, *Moby-Dick* is a book about water, and Melville is to me a more reliable guide than all the denizens of a faculty lounge. "Say you are in the country," he writes. "Take any path you please, and ten to one it carries you down in a dale, and leaves you there by a pool in the stream." He goes on: "Let the most absent-minded of men be plunged in his deepest reveries—stand that man on his legs, set his feet a-going, and he will infallibly lead you to water. . . . Yes, as every one knows, meditation and water are wedded for ever."

The wonderful mystery that there are fish at all is the angler's first meditation. That something as beautiful as trout inhabit something as beautiful as a trout stream is a coincidence of inexpressibly good fortune, and just the kind of thing you can steer by. Cross-country hikers and orienteers know well the limits of map and compass, that magnetic declinations can draw you off the path. But a trout stream is an agonic line where compass readings are always faithful, and a fly rod points as truly as any radish.

9

Down to Zero

Where is the summer, the unimaginable

zero summer?

—*T.S. Eliot, "Little Gidding"*

The Deschutes again. The circus has left town, its only vestiges the crumbling shucks of long-gone salmonflies and empty husks of paper and aluminum cast off by departing campers, exuvia of the hatch now dessicating in a summer sun. The desert air grows hard and dry as a white stone. The tenuous greens of spring fade from the slopes, trickling downhill and collecting in the narrow fringe of vegetation that still thrives at the river's edge. Under a cloudless sky, the landscape browns like a baking loaf.

Days lengthen into indefiniteness. In scrubby draws, quail and chukar hide out. Coyotes sleep in dens. Trout hug the shady banks and the shadowed lees of rocks, waiting for evening.

In this steep country, the sun sets prematurely, dropping early below the high butte on Webster Flat. But the day itself lingers in the heat rising from volcanic dust, the resinous odor of sagebrush, and in the glow of the rimrock still lit by the sun. Through a long dusk, light climbs the ochre and gray canyon rocks and is mirrored in the river hundreds of feet below, suffusing the landscape from top to bottom with a golden-bronze light that tints whatever it touches. You wade in the reflection of a reflection, and the coppery water streams against your legs like something molten.

It is a serenely beautiful light, but damned hard to see in. Standing shin-deep among thick, wavering tendrils of ranunculus, I can just make out a pair of geese herding four goslings to the point of the island for the night. Caddis flutter everywhere, lighting on the back of my hands and crawling over my glasses. In the dim metallic twilight, the first few rings appear, expanding concentric zeros of rising trout. They are barely perceptible on the riffly seam between the channel and flats, like intermittent bits of sense snatched from radio static. Fly and tippet raised in silhouette against the sky, I work in two dimensions to thread one to the other and eventually manage a questionable knot.

Before long the river is spattered with rises, vague bullseyes I can't seem to hit because I can't see where my fly lands. The last light settles on the river in a pale cross-current streak, and as on so many June evenings before, I wade up or down to center this foot-wide window of lightness over a few working fish, their ripples black against the faint flush. The casts are guesses of distance and drift, and I strike at every rise. Mostly there's just empty air and a headstart on the next backcast, but now and again, I meet the resistance of something solid that surges without pause to the middle of the river and leaps in the darkness. A big trout here—and most of them are—will instantly quarter down and out, and gaining the main current, can spool you in half a minute. Long before that, this one breaks the leader.

On other days, I'd stick with it, losing at last the dwindling June light and fishing by sense and sound. Tonight, without the pang of opportunity foregone, I wade out and watch the last of the rises, and beyond them the long, unruffled expanse of a summer that will gloss these first few hours.

At an early age I more or less consciously concluded that the things I was really interested in possessing could only be bought with time, not money, and that I would make it my business to trade the one for the other whenever possible. Whether this implied a kind of wisdom or a kind of laziness is a question I've always sensed wouldn't bear much scrutiny. Nevertheless, in the cunning, Confucian way that life sometimes works itself out, I seem to have been given precisely what I'd asked for. I have at my disposal more uncommitted time than is ordinarily considered seemly for an adult, whereas money remains largely a theoretical concept. All in all, the circumstance is only slightly more equivocal than I supposed it would be.

The exact moment all this dawned on me is distinctly clear in my memory—a warm early-June morning at my grandmother's house in the farm country of southern Wisconsin. I was ten. School had let out the day before. I was sitting in a backyard that sloped and then leveled its way to the banks of Turtle Creek, a sluggish little mudhole that at the time I regarded as the most fascinating body of water on earth. It was for many years a place where I would inflict my curiosity on toads, frogs, chubs, crayfish, and all the usual victims of childhood's wanton and sadistic wonder.

Thinking of nothing at all, really, but lying in the cool, uncut grass, feeling the fineness of the day and how much of it lay ahead, I was struck immediately and altogether, the way a sonic boom seems to hit you with a pressure wave from all sides at once, that it wasn't just the promise of the creek that waited before me, or even the rest of the day, but the day after, and the day after that, stretching on into a distance I could scarcely contemplate. It wasn't some sudden first grip on the concept of "summer"—that, I understood entirely—rather, I was seized by the intuition of perfect open-endedness, the vision of a vast uncluttered plain of time over which my existence would move without keel or destination, frictionlessly propelled by the slightest puffs of whim or desire. The force of this awareness detonated in my mind a soft implosion of pure bliss that ran through me like a transfusion. A poor man's infinity, I suppose, but it was plenty to handle then, as it is now.

This sense of unfetteredness, of the future as a patient infinity, was for summer after summer a free-floating thing, though not a neutral one. It was charged like an ion, and the year I turned sixteen, drew into its orbit the attractive prospects of a driver's license and a not-so-nearby trout stream. My vast plain of time suddenly acquired a topography of hills and meadows, highways and gravel roads, open rivers and weedy spring creeks. The vista of summer changed from simply all-the-time-in-the-world to the decidedly more particular all-the-time-in-the-world-to-fish. Or so it seemed at first. Trout fishing, I was to learn, was a season. It had an opening, but it also had a closing, and this little-expected development significantly altered the view. My sense of open-endedness began to acquire the finitude of its object, as the onset of the trout season already implied its finish. I went at every conceivable opportunity. The fishing was often good and the days immensely happy, though now touched with a consciousness of their extent, in just the way that all powerful emotions seem to me now tinged with their opposites. At the time, I was well aware that things die, had even some notion of death, but this particular feeling of an end lurking within the fact of beginning was for a while the most palpable understanding I had of mortality.

September was the wall, the close of the season as incomprehensibly laid down by the Department of Natural Resources. It deposited me on the edge of a great black void, of eight-and-a-half lightless months of winter with nothing to hold on to but the none-too-sure conviction that next summer, another season would come. In the interim were the small facts of eternity and gym class. By December, I was deeply depressed; by April, given to minor psychotic episodes and kept marginally sedated by the narcotics of anticipation and tackle catalogs. When the trout streams finally opened, the soul-rinsing relief was inexpressible.

Though I eventually moved West for much different reasons, I have come to appreciate this one above all others: It rescued me from seasons. They exist here, to be sure, but less as a matter of calendars than of inclination and opportunity. Salmon, winter steelhead, whitefish, trout, shad, spring chinook, trout, smallmouth, summer steelhead, sea-run cutthroat, salmon—they overlap like the scales of fish, layered three and four deep on some rivers, the smooth skin of a year that is proof against a good many things. You fish with a psychic tilt, listing forward, the momentum of one season bearing you into the next, and the sense is overwhelmingly of beginning rather than ending.

It's a personal version of a cultural idea, I suppose—the West as a place of starting over, of renewal, a world always on the verge of opening out. Oregon was, and is, my "fresh green breast of the new world," though it grows a little less green every day. But outfitted with an open mind, warm waders, and semireliable transportation, it is possible to step into a consecutive series of new beginnings and, with the right kind of eyes, to see precisely the rarity there to be appreciated.

The sudden liberation from a sense of seasonal boundaries had two entirely serendipitous, if slightly contradictory, consequences. Old habits die hard, and some not at all. The lengthening days of summer for so long marked the onset of the fishing season that I found myself unable to abandon the idea altogether. Though I may have fished almost continuously for twelve months running, summer remains a psychological beginning. It is the newest start in this place of new starts, the zero point of my year.

And from here I survey the summer, and this summer in particular, in much the old way, as a horizon of pure possibility of indefinite tenure with a nearly ridiculous personal liberty and an unshackled sense of the lightness of existence. Summer shapes itself in my mind as a zero-gravity world where rivers and lakes, fly rods and landscapes, trout and highways, whim, will, happenstance, and all the time in the world drift freely, bumping gently together in endlessly recombinant and deeply pleasurable collisions.

When your chief engagement with the world of commerce is exchanging money for time, dollars become days. And lying in the cool, uncut grass on the bank of the Deschutes, I contemplate the venture capital of a summer's happiness stretched out before me, an unnumbered Swiss account of unnumbered sunny days that I intend to spend to the last nickel. I don't even mind squandering some. Like a lottery winner lighting victory cigars with a hundred-dollar bill, I burn a little time just watching the last few rises to the last few caddis on this first of evenings, and look forward to a summer as exquisitely functionless as the fishing that will fill it.

New waters or old? That is the summer question. They're filed side-by-side in a fisherman's mind like shelves of books. Some are familiar and well-thumbed, the favorite parts underlined with notes in the margin; stood on their spines, they fall open to the places you can quote from memory. Fishing them offers the delights of rereading—the intimacy of things already known and the small, subtle surprises of discovery within the familiar. Beside them are new lakes and streams, unknown quantities temptingly jacketed and attractively titled, loaned by friends or picked up on a hunch, their waters waiting to be read.

Deciding not to decide, I take down some of each. And as all rivers do, each eventually clarifies itself as one of the infinite variations on the single theme of moving water, the simplest of all ideas in countless permutation that makes all rivers at once perfectly individual and essentially alike. In incidental echoes, river is linked to river, event to event. They overlap, contacting at capricious points, coincidences of memory and sense—the sharp smell of sagebrush, the ratchet of a kingfisher, the feel of a hot wind or a heavy trout in the hand—until you cannot seize hold of one without the rest clinging to it.

Time, someone once said, is what keeps everything from happening at once. Its medium is motion, constant and cyclonic, in which events are held separate by the sheer force of ongoingness, like leaves in a fall whirlwind. Against the pressure of a summer sun, time slows; movement slackens; and the grains of recollection settle out into the thin, intervalless lamina of simultaneity.

Below Leaburg Dam, the south bank of the McKenzie River climbs steeply and is matched in pitch by the long wooden slide that sluices a boat from a small pull-off down forty feet to the river, or somewhere thereabouts. It looks like an old log flume and, on a dew-slick morning like this one, functions with the same ungovernable approximateness. The launch can be a ticklish business by yourself, but this morning it is uneventful.

With their usual mandarin inscrutability, the Eugene Water & Electric people have cranked down the gates despite a recent rain. The water is low, and bedrock ribs and vertebrae poke everywhere through the skin of the river. It promises to be a rocky ride—not the bucking stuff of whitewater, but an occasional African-Queen-style boat drag over gravelly shoals and stone shelves. I tie a line to the bow before pushing off and then dodge my way downriver between the rocks and the aluminum skid marks left by other low-water drifters.

Half-a-mile down, the water splits and files through three parallel slots, as uniform as furrows in the riverbed. The sun hasn't yet cleared the firs on the bank, and in the morning shade, I fish through a sequence of nymphs—#14 Hare's Ear on the point, #16 Pheasant Tail on the dropper; point fly off, #14 Muskrat on; dropper off, #18 Black A.P. on; point off. . . . It has all the appearance of a random exploration, but I know in advance exactly where it's all headed, the way you can spiral down to the point in a conversation, to prolong the pleasure or defer disappointment, knowing from the start you'll eventually get there.

I end up where I thought. On the dropper is a #16 Green Sparkle Pupa, a pattern that is sheer inspiration on some rivers, a waste of time on others, and a #14 Zug Bug on the point, a fly that has caught hundreds of trout for me, but one for which I haven't developed the slightest bit of affection. Immediately, I begin mopping up on little ones—small cutthroats, steelhead and salmon smolts—each a wonderfully precise miniature of what it may someday become.

With a few firm exceptions, fishing from boats holds little appeal. It has a certain industrial quality about it, a no-nonsense fixation on the business of catching fish, and I'd much rather drift from place to place, working the promising water on foot, which brings you closer to everything. Sometimes, though, casting from a boat can't be helped. The slower, unwadable pools are tinted a translucent emerald and transected by solid columns of light that exaggerate the sense of the water's depth. To a short leader and a sink-tip line, I tie an undesignated miscellany of marabou and hen hackle and chuck the whole unruly mess to one side, feeding line until fly and boat are synchronized in the same lazy drift. The technique is as craven as it sounds, modeled after the drift fisherman's practice of "boondoggling," a corruption of the term "boom-dogging," that came about in earlier times when long rafts of logs were herded down rivers. The tag ends of huge chains that bound the booms together dragged the river bottoms and stirred up everything, including the steelhead. Boat fishermen would follow (or "dog") the booms in hopes of finding takers among the agitated fish. With a distinctly regional penchant for the heavy-duty, boom-dogging was a cross between stoning the pool and the world's biggest San Juan shuffle, with all the genteel attraction of hunting pheasants behind a grain combine.

I set the rod down and, working under the assumption that an empty bladder is the devil's workshop, open a beer, hand-picked for the day and requiring the reassuring inconvenience of a bottle opener. Only a stout can measure up to the intensity of a summer noon, and Grant's Imperial, the issue of a Washington microbrewery, is nothing if not intense. It pours like used motor oil, has a potent bitterness and enough body to make solid food redundant. Not exactly the stuff one swills by the six-pack, it takes an hour to drink one properly, perhaps a bit longer with the hard-smoked trout I've packed along with it.

History being what it is, I count myself lucky to have been born into an age of renaissance in both fly fishing and serious brewing. In the right proportion, they resonate with unusual harmony in the pace and subtlety of their enjoyment. That some varieties of beer blend especially well with certain types of trout water seems to me a book-worthy subject, though the world is not yet ready for this. Or so I was told by a publisher to whom I mentioned the idea—over, incidentally, a tap of Blackhook Porter, the hands-down beverage for any editorial negotiation.

In mid-sip, the rod tip plunges deeply twice, strains to some invisible surge, and, before I can swallow, springs straight under a limp line and clatters hollowly against the gunnel. It is no less than I deserve.

On a day in late August, you don't need a physicist to tell you that light exerts pressure. You can feel it on your shoulders and the back of your neck, a pleasant weight that induces the kind of reverie always and best described as "thinking about nothing." I ship the oars and sip the beer. Unchecked, the boat drifts to an eddy on the left bank and idles there in slow, counterclockwise revolution, suspended beneath the long pause of a windless afternoon.

On a windless afternoon, I climb the flank of a canyon along a small coastal stream, shown to me years ago by a friend in exchange for the promise never to reveal its location. His caution, however understandable, was unnecessary. The 30% grade of crumbling rock, the pathless descent through a tangle of deadfalls, scrub, and dense patches of Himalaya vine have so far proven more than adequate to safeguard the place.

Nine hours ago, I picked my way down the slope with high hopes and a daypack to the little freestone creek. Its bouldery bed, brisk runs, plunge pools, and deep basinlike holes brought to mind similar streams I'd only recently left behind in the Blue Ridge and Allegheny Mountains of Virginia. Instead of wild brook trout, I found native coastal cutthroats, though in their way these two fishes are as much alike as the streams they inhabit. The cutts are small, beautifully formed fish with opalescent bellies, silver sides, and blue-green backs flushed with violet, indigo, and red. The orange slash beneath their gills is precisely the color of a spawning brook trout and, like them, the cutthroats are quick and nervous, but aggressive if not spooked, with a fondness for bright flies and shady water.

On my first trip to a coastal stream, I was struck by the similarity of the two species and of the places they are fished. And I still take pleasure in the accidental symmetry: The native brook trout of the ancient Appalachians and the wild cutthroats of the young Pacific Coast Range bookend the continent and bracket the world of my trout fishing.

The fish come easily, one or two ten-inch cutts from each little run and pool, jabbing fiercely against a resilient six-foot cane rod, lovingly if amateurishly built from the top two sections of an old Granger Favorite I bought for $8 at a rummage sale. I catch dozens of trout in the slow passage upstream. Scrambling over boulders, crisscrossing the water, wading through thick stands of ferns, trillium, wood sorrel, and wild bleeding heart that flourish in the damp shade, I travel three miles for every one of river, and once, boosting myself over a deadfall, settle my butt in banana slug half again as long as my hand.

Sitting on the shank of a fallen cedar, I eat lunch (a pair of stream-chilled Cold Spring Exports and a cellophane bag of some kind of cheese things). The trunk is massive, perhaps sixteen feet in circumference, and the root mass suggests it fell some time before the area was first logged at the turn of the century. Such a tree would never have escaped axe and oxen. The surface is bleached and smooth as whitened bone, but cedar endures like the mountains, and there is little doubt that beneath the weathering, its wood is sound and fragrant, good for another century at least. In the pool backed up by the deadfall, I soothe barked shins and wash the slug slime off my jeans.

The frothy water spilling into the head of this pool produces the largest trout of the day, a skinny thirteen-inch fish that I imagine was seeing its last season. Not many weeks before, in water much like this, I discovered the fresh carcass of a giant Pacific salamander, a prehistoric-looking creature a full foot long with a broad flattened head and tiny eyes. On a hunch, I wade the edges of the pool, poking among rocks and leaves, looking for a live one. Instead, under a sheet of peeled bark are two enormous millipedes with thick, hard, deeply segmented bodies, like finger-length sections of a gooseneck lamp.

They are a prefiguration. A month later on Fall River, the trout we've come for, big browns alleged to haunt the lower stretches, are apparently haunting someplace else, though we manage a few in the three- to four-inch class. Wading out for a rest, I upend an unsplit fire log for a seat and expose, amid the dust and rotting bark, two families of black widows. A pair of obsidian females scutters among several dozen small spiders, already with the distinctive body shape but not yet black, their abdomens a mottled glossy brown like tumbled agates. They seem as little inclined to bite as the fish.

Fall River cuts through the flows of basalt laid on the leveling slope of the eastern Cascades, and the stream threads its way among stands of fir and Ponderosa. Much of it is shallow, flowing thinly over sandy, troutless bottom and offers holding water only behind the many bankside sweepers. But it is one of the best places I know to see birds. There are tanagers here in enormous numbers, and from forest floor to canopy, woodpeckers drill incessantly.

Toward afternoon, I hook the only real fish of the day, a rainbow that darts from beneath a volcanic ledge to grab a nymph almost at my feet. Its thrashings on the surface of the narrow channel attract the notice of an osprey peering over the edge of a jackstraw nest built in a Ponderosa snag. The bird rocks for a moment on the edge of indecision, tempted by an easy meal but concluding, eventually, that I'm a little too close.

Sixty miles and six weeks away, the osprey on Davis Lake are not nearly so timid. Wings and tails flared to stall against the incoming breeze, they perch in freeze-frame on an invisible column of air and scan the water below. Then folding up, they spear fifty feet of air and shatter the lake amid casting fishermen and dimpling trout, taking fish one dive out of three and preening their feathers between tries. Six birds work the small lake at the same time.

The water is almost as clear as the air (all this before the lake was poisoned for rough fish), and pods of whitefish swim beneath the boat to forage among the reed beds like schools of mudding bonefish. Trout are mixed in, too—rainbows, some going six or eight pounds. We fish the margin of the weeds with 6X tippet and a tiny Pheasant Tail or Cates Turkey, studying the precise point where the leader slips beneath the surface film, waiting for the nervous flutter that may signal a take. We work hand-twist retrieves with a patient, glacial crawl that makes lake fishing, at best, the sport of monks and at worst a barbiturate daze. I venture this opinion after hours beneath a blazing afternoon—that river fishing is inherently more interesting, exacting more skill and invention, better for the soul and eye, less stultifying and more productive.

Later that night I dine on these words, and though well-spiced with irony and served with a clean Sierra Nevada Bock, they taste remarkably like crow. For at twilight, ginger midges appear. The lake is alive with rises, and from sunset to insensibility, we twitch #18 Blond Haystacks to quick, hard hits.

By the time it is over we need flashlights to beach the boat in the shallows beside camp. As the bow slides to a stop in the silt, the shoreline seems suddenly to dissolve in a quick, diffuse shiver, and just as quickly coalesce to solidity. In one of the more curious, small-potatoes spectacles I've seen, the beach is blanketed with a swarm of tiny toads that jump in unison at the sound of the boat. Each is a duplicate of the next, knobby, ambered-eyed halves-of-an-inch, the color of an old penny. A score of them would fit in a boot-track, and I skirt the shore for a quarter mile, each footstep sending up an explosive little cloud of toads. They must number in the tens of thousands.

They brought to mind the grasshoppers on the Williamson River—the same flurried, cross-hatched scattering, a net of movement cast in the grass to trap the eye with confusion. Hordes of them clicked like mussels in the sun. I took the hint and twitched small hopper patterns on twelve-foot leaders in the glassy stretches below Spring Creek, avoiding the meat bucket at Chiloquin and, it turned out, most of the trout.

Not a whisper of air disturbed the blank, blistering August afternoon that bridged the two ends of this very buggy day. In the morning chill, I sat in a camper with a steaming mug of coffee, watching hundreds of *Tricos* molting outside on the window glass, and waited for a spinner fall that never came. I fished hoppers during the hot afternoon, and dusk came with the audible, aggregate whine of a million mosquitos.

One of them sank an exploratory shaft into an already tender and inflamed swelling next to my watch band, and I hoped it was poisoned by residual venom. A few days before, at 7:20 P.M., while I was wading the North Umpqua, minding my own affairs, a sudden burning in my wrist triggerd a violent, involuntary, full-body spasm. A yellow jacket lazily flew off from a reddening circle beside the winding stem of a watch that read 7:20. I dipped my arm in the cold water for half a minute, but couldn't spare more. Caddis were hatching all around me, and from bank to bank the river was pocked with rises.

I had come, as all do, to fish this holiest of water for steelhead. I cast without conviction when the sun was high, but in the evening, with the river blanketed in shadows and caddis, I began to think I might have blundered upon every steelhead fisherman's sweetest dream—the chance to take a bright sea-run fish on a dry fly and light trout tackle. Knotting on an Elk Hair Caddis, I dressed it with flotant and hope and covered rise after rise, beginning with the near bank and working slowly outward among deceptively swift currents and rocks of legendary slickness.

In the end, the steelheader's dream remained just that, but I caught some cutthroats, a few decently large, and fished the caddis, to me among the most agreeable of all hatches.

For reasons both historical and aesthetic, the mayfly is angling's glamor-bug. It garners most of the press and a lavish attention from fly tyers. No single group of insects has spawned more or more various patterns than the mayfly, from nymphs to spinners to the hyper-refinements of crippled emergers and stillborn duns. A mayfly is never just a mayfly. Show a single Pale Morning Dun to any serious fisherman, and he'll give you the full breakdown in an instant: *Ephemerella inermis*; #17 female imago; recently molted; slightly more reddish than the norm; with egg sac. Venture that it's a "little rusty mayfly" and you'll be hooted out of the corps. Our exactness defers as much to their beauty as necessity.

But most of the time, a caddis is just a caddis—maybe a "speckled caddis" or a "little black caddis," and it seldom goes much beyond that. Nevertheless, I have an abiding fondness for caddis and regard them as the preeminent fly of summer—reliable and prolific, an everyday workhorse, the utility outfielder of bugs. Were it a beer, it would Henry Weinhard's or Rolling Rock. Few insects can match the elegance of a mayfly, as precise and delicate as an origami bird. The caddis, however, is a fisherman's fly.

Though mostly dull grays and tans, some are strikingly patterned, and of these, none more so than a caddis I saw first when I came west—a big fly, an inch long, with tawny wings grained in shades of chestnut and gold, like a chip of burnished oak. Quite by accident, I came to know them better in a freshly painted outhouse at a campsite on the middle Deschutes. There on the wall, above a roll of toilet paper, wings and legs and antennae perfectly and symmetrically extended, one of these caddis had become stuck in the paint and dried there, every translucent detail of its anatomy visible over the background of pure white. Underneath it, in the neat, squared hand of a draftsman, was printed, "*Hesperophylax incisus*." Back at the tent, I fetched a thick volume of aquatic entomology and returned to the privy, passing a group of rafters whose looks questioned just what I had in mind and just how long it was going to take. I found the identification accurate.

Some time later, I discovered the caption was the job of someone I distantly knew. Much of life depends from such coincidences. Despite our efforts to plot the cause and effect of events, history seems to rattle from one accident to another in a pachinko of chance associations.

Which is how I happen to be sitting on the South Jetty of Yaquina Bay, with the butt of an eleven-foot surf rod wedged in the rocks beside me. The first outdoor magazine I ever saw fell into my hands thirty years ago, and I read it at once from cover to cover, including a pair of run-of-the-mill fishing yarns that knit themselves together in my mind. The first concerned catching large trout on small flies and featured an inset photo of a gigantic rainbow with a tiny midge nearly invisible in its huge maw. The second was about surf-casting and pictured a lone angler in waders carrying an enormous red drum by the gill plates, its tail dragging in the sand of a deserted beach. The images were instantly and permanently yoked together. I'd never fly fished, and surf was a little hard to come by in Wisconsin, so I recognized no particular incongruity. Thirty years later, the one idea still clings compatibly to the other, following it around instinctively like one of Konrad Lorenz's geese, and the fact that it's only a synaptic fluke doesn't bother me.

Soaking chunks of mussel on the bottom of the bay, I'm hoping for ling cod (several months out of season); I'll take anything I can get. Today, it happens to be a few sculpins, a small rockfish, and a nice Dungeness crab that surrenders the bait before I can nab it. The wind shifts on the ebb tide and mounts nearly a full gale by afternoon. At the juncture of outgoing tidal currents and onshore gusts, the mouth of the jetty develops a heavy chop and dangerous rips. Charters wait offshore for a lull, then hurry in. I cast in the same lulls, but the power of the wind and plumes of cold spray drive me off. At home, I steam the rest of the mussels.

I fished in wind like this once on Chickahominy Lake, the kind of muddy, bleak, weather-whipped toilet I've seen only in eastern Oregon. One comes here strictly for the fishing, though often enough that is sufficient. In the morning, I was pinned inside my tent by a Hereford bull grazing the campsite; in the afternoon, my back to roaring wind, I cast stiffly to the tips of sunken sagebrush and caught fat rainbows on lethally weighted Woolly Buggers.

I drill one of these same flies into my ear on a breezy morning fishing the North Santiam. Daubing at a remarkable quantity of blood leaking from my ear lobe, I walk back to the car for some lunch, a sclerosis of bacon and avocado on pumpernickel and a bottle of Mt. Hood Hefeweizen, a thin, cloudy gruel of a beer made from wheat. But it chills well and takes the edge off a hot day. Laying out these provisions on the steel siderail of the bridge, I watch a fisherman in voluminous chest waders on the far bank, half-hidden in the shadow of the concrete abutment. He's holding a spinning rod bent nearly in half by the exertions of an apparently large fish in the deep, heavy current sweeping beneath the bridge.

When he looks up, I can tell he's shouting something, but the sound is lost in the rush of the river and in the rattles and grumbles of an ancient flatbed truck, headed my way down the edge of a vast field of strawberries. The engine stops, a door slams, and I'm joined on the bridge by the driver, an Hispanic farm laborer in his mid-fifties perhaps, with a skin like weathered elk hide and the broad cheekbones and nose I've seen in Mayan stone reliefs. He taps an open cigarette pack against his lower lip with a practiced gesture that slides out a single smoke just far enough to grab with his teeth, and lights it. By the fit of his work glove, I can tell he's missing the little finger of his right hand.

The fisherman below is clearly losing ground. A formidable chute runs between the midriver bridge piling and the concrete abutment on the bank that is blocking his passage downriver. The rod tip lunges rhythmically; each pulse exacts a squealing little burp from the reel and moves the fish a few feet farther away. From the other side of the bridge, we make out the flash of a sizeable steelhead, bright as a new dime and twisting in the current. No more than a hundred feet below the fish, the river gathers to the right and drops through a whitewater sluice that curves against an evil-looking rip-rap bank.

The driver smokes, I finish my sandwich and sip the beer, and it's obvious to both of us that the thing is about over, when the fisherman tugs at the drawstrings on his waders, raises his rod above his head with both hands, and steps into the channel. The river laps at his neck, though it is not as deep as I thought. He bobs downstream with just enough control to stay upright but not enough to influence his speed or direction, and disappears under the bridge.

Touching the cigarette for the first time with his muddy glove, my companion flicks an exclamatory ash and quietly exhales, "Cojones."

I respond with equal understatement, a stifled swallow and aborted laugh that ejects a fine spray of wheat beer out each nostril. This hurts, but amuses him highly, and we hurry to the other side of the bridge.

On schedule, the fisherman reappears, feebly sweeping his right arm to draw him to the bank. His circumstance is not yet dangerous, but getting there. Opening the bail on his reel to release line, he clamps the rod butt crosswise in his teeth and begins the clumsy dogpaddle of a man in swamped waders. At the edge of the current, he regains some footing and tightens the line, but the fish has already hit the tongue of the sluice and the monofilament parts like a rifle shot.

It is impossible to walk in brimful waders. Instead, the fisherman crawls on his hands and knees to the banks and bows his head to the ground. A few gallons of the North Santiam spill from his wader tops, and from our angle, he looks remarkably like a man puking. Stretching full-length on the bank, he slides his feet uphill to drain out the rest of the water and for a moment doesn't move. Then he reaches to his breast pocket, and with superb insouciance, puts on a pair of sunglasses and folds his hands neatly across his stomach.

My companion spits his cigarette into the river and returns to the flatbed. I drive upstream to Fisherman's Bend and creel a handful of hatchery trout with a death wish. That evening, I brine and smoke them, and will eat them in a few days, drifting down the McKenzie with a Grant's Imperial Stout beneath a windless afternoon.

Summer is as much a space as it is a time, though in the end these things behave in much the same fashion. In the bright, flat light of midday summer (the one shunned by photographers and painters), space collapses. Perspective-giving shadows shrink and with them the distinctions of remoteness and proximity. The landscape forfeits dimension as foreground and background merge, and the scene becomes as depthless as a canvas. It's a trick of the light, but what things are not?

The same sun beats down a sense of simple aliveness powerful enough to stop a clock. Time folds in on itself. Events are superimposed, an endless succession of images on a single emulsion that reproduces no space between then and now. Time telescopes into itself, and could you cross-section a season, summer would show the concentric rings of a tree trunk, expanding iterations of an archetype, like a riseform.

And like a riseform, summer pleases best in the evening. It is a curious fact of perception that the architecture of a summer day is not symmetrical. An astronomer, citing the constancy of bodies in space, can prove to you that the climb of a morning sun to the meridian and its descent to the western horizon are nearly mirror images of one another. They are equivalent events; a sunset is merely a sunrise played backward. But nothing could be further from the sense of these things. In a lifetime of fishing, I've watched thousands of sunrises, many of them more striking than sunsets, but their beauty is, above all else, momentary and transitory. The first soft flush of dawn hardens without pause to the light of common day. The rise of the sun is sudden and summary, no sooner begun than finished, a beautiful but businesslike preliminary to the business end of the day, its advance as headlong and steady as a cesium clock. I have never seen a lingering dawn.

But it is the essence of a sunset to linger. In imperceptible gradations, it fades to the indefinite and suspended duration of twilight, and dusk feels less an ending than an onset.

The geometry of a summer day is not a perfect hemisphere. It curves eccentrically and elongates time. There is a bulge in the day at evening, as there is in the year at summer, and it is shaped like the bend of the fly rod in my hand, arced to a trout that will in a moment break free into the dimming, gold-leaf currents of the Deschutes, where I will watch the last few rises to the last few caddis, down to zero, on a summer-solstice evening, at the best part of the best part of the year.

10

<hr/>

Seeing the Elephant

<hr/>

Mr. Plornish amiably growled, in his philosophical but not lucid

manner, that there was ups you see, and there was downs. It

was in vain to ask why ups, why downs; there they was, you

know. He had heerd it given for a truth that accordin' as

the world went round, which round it did rewolve undoubted,

even the best of gentlemen must take his turn of standing

with his ed upside down and all his air a flying the wrong

way into what you might call Space.

—*Charles Dickens*, Little Dorrit

At the far end of a reclining lawn chair, my right foot is propped on pillows under the August sun, superimposed on the backdrop of a trout stream, an emblem of something. I study the spectrum of a painfully swollen big toe—subtle violets, midnight indigos, a ghastly yellow fading to a blush of inflammatory red—as if overnight my right foot has sprouted a fully ripened Italian plum. Framed by a break in the alders, it seems a painting: "Still Life with Gout." And it still is.

People invariably find this funny, and I've grown immune to their wry little smirks and witty reproaches about rich living, pointing out that the affliction has a long and prominent, if not altogether noble, history. Admittedly, the great scoundrel and libertine Henry VIII suffered from gout, but so did the epic genius, Milton, who died of complications from it. There are hints that it plagued Alexander Pope, whose poetry is considered the greatest ever written by an acerbic eighteenth-century homunculus. And in our own time, the stricken epicure Calvin Trillin has written persuasively on the subject. (Gout is also said to be the most common disease in the U.S. Senate, a fact that we on the inside don't generally spread around.)

I felt the familiar, premonitory twinges in the joint of my toe last night, and immediately washed down a preemptive pill with a mouthful of Sierra Nevada Porter, the only strictly utilitarian swallow of the evening. It was an empty gesture, vain and self-defeating, since beer is to gout as mobile-home parks are to tornadoes. The natural affinity is indisputable, and I woke in the morning as you see me now. The group of old friends, whose arrival occasioned the evening's intemperance, wear their own hangovers lightly in deference to my condition, and this thoughtfulness, along with a vial of Demarol in my shirt pocket, soothes the sting a little. I'd waited months to bring these particular friends to my favorite river in the peak season and fish with them on its best and most beautiful stretches. Now, sitting alone, I can only sight down my swollen toe like a transit and survey all the water I'm not fishing.

The universe may, as science tells us, be composed of subatomic building blocks, but I suspect that irony is the mortar that holds them together. For no apparent reason, fate springs a handstand, inverting circumstance, momentarily turning the world into its opposite. In nature, the reversal produces vaguely disturbing anomalies. On the Williamson River, not far from the headless ex-volcano of Crater Lake, you sometimes come across rocks that float, foamy fist-sized chunks of pumice that bob in eddies and eerily nudge your leg. In the ordinary course of things, eagles, osprey, herons, and gulls thrive on fish. But at the nodes of inversion, fish eat birds; in the shallows of northern lakes, big muskie and pike lurk like alligators among the weeds and gobble down ducks. Trout capture insects, but there are insects that catch trout, water scorpions that ambush alevins, and green darners hovering like Hueys, snatching up fry. Some streams, gripped in anchor ice, freeze strangely from the bottom up.

Every angler has his private litany of hapless turns of fortune and inexplicable synaptic misfires—the carefully prepared wallet of shooting heads that you remember, in midstream, sits at home on the kitchen table; the hatch that fails to come off under perfect conditions; the abrupt appearance of a funny noise from the engine; the broken rod, completely forgotten, until it's uncased at the river on opening day; the sudden conviction, six hours from home, that you left the coffee pot on; trips that began in soaring euphoria and, under bad weather, bad fishing, or bad luck, crashed like the Hindenburg. And, of course, gout. These, I suppose, should be expected, reflecting the general proclivity of fate, when all is going well, to bound from the shadows swinging a sand-filled length of rubber hose. You try to muster a little grace is all.

At some level, though, fishing becomes concerned with catching things other than fish. It assumes in the psyche the shape of longing, and perhaps in its own modest way, even the lineaments of a quest. This deeper impulse is the most engaging dimension of any passion. It is also the most equivocal. Astride his horse Rocinante, Don Quixote fixed his eye inexorably on windmills ahead, while the dusty road behind was strewn with heaps of Rocinante's own antiromantic inevitabilities.

As with all matters of the soul, fishing has the perverse capacity for spiritual backfire, and at times does exactly that. Over the years, I've tried to introduce a number of people to fly fishing, not so much to teach them about catching fish (though this was always part of it) but to steer them as best I could to the source of its more elusive attractions and its subtle power to sustain. To name the thing properly, I suppose, I was out to convert rather than instruct. No matter that it succeeds in fishing about as well as it does in anything else. We'd launch a boat and drift a river, and I would eagerly point out a thousand particulars, each a concentrated reason and compressed meaning—the mosaic of cobbles on a riverbed, a rising trout, nymphs scuttling on the underside of a river rock, an emerging mayfly dun, the way currents fan over a dark and promising pool. Certain profundities defy explication, and confronted by them, as the great teacher Lionel Trilling once observed, you are reduced to the primitive function of pointing and admiring, which is what I did.

You can acquire the technical skills of fly fishing, but the fishing temperament is something you're born with. A few of my companions had it and readily appreciated what they saw in and on the river and understood that these things were essentially self-explanatory. Most people did not, and though they politely enjoyed themselves, they never saw what all the fuss was about, which is hardly cause for regret. There are other things to live for. But once or twice, as I was on the verge of pointing to some particular and exclaiming, "Do you see? *That* is why I fish," the whole undertaking, for no apparent reason, simply reversed polarity. Trying to convey some sense of the importance that inhered in details, I was instead overcome by an awareness of how inconsequential and slight a thing my faith hung on. Urging them to see through my eyes, I saw instead through theirs. The significance I invested and the tiny occasions for it seemed absurdly disproportionate and joined by only the most tenuous ligature of conviction. No newly hatched mayfly could ever lift off the water bearing the weight of meaning I attached to it, and I was struck by the distinct possibility for breakdown.

One hundred and fifty years ago, migrants on the westward trail rallied round a slogan that taunted fate: "Oregon or Bust." Those for whom "Bust" was a surer destiny than "Oregon" developed a second expression—"seeing the elephant." One day, they would simply and suddenly be seized by a revelation of the impossible enormity of what lay ahead, an insuperable and malign grayness with an impenetrable hide, a colossal resistance that trampled the will. They saw the elephant and turned back. Physical adversity may have been the occasion, but a desertion of spirit was the cause.

Fishing has its elephants too. Some days, you're done long before you ever stop. A point arrives when fishing turns into casting, and casting devolves into empty and mechanical reflex that barely registers on consciousness, the way a word repeated over and over in your mind becomes only a droning of senseless, unfamiliar syllables. You're most apt to see the elephant on those occasions when everything converges on the trout and catching them reduces to a species of necessity. Intending only to anchor hope and anticipation in something tangible, you end up setting expectation like a snare. When the fish don't come, as sometimes they don't, you grasp, all at once, the comic sense of scale, the cosmic disparity between the volume of water in front of you and the ridiculously small fly with which you are attempting to "search" it. In the mind's eye appears an aerial photograph—a vast expanse of blank water surrounding a randomly placed, subatomic speck bearing the tiny label, "Your fly is here," with an arrow. In the face of that kind of futility, another cast is almost unbearable.

Despite what we think we understand about rivers and lakes, they hide what they know with remarkable ease. I have twice unknowingly fished poisoned water, once on a small spring creek slightly less vital, but more dear to me, than an artery. A negligent farmer and a not-terribly-large drum of pesticide annihilated everything downstream of the spill. The second time, in the Potholes region of southwest Washington, the lake had been rotenoned and every fish exterminated in the name of the fishery.

In both instances, I fished as hopefully as always. True, there were no signs of fish anywhere, but this is frequently the case under ordinary circumstances. I tried fly after fly, place after place, and caught nothing, which is also frequently the case. And precisely the point. There was simply no way of knowing I was committed to something so thoroughly meaningless.

Later, when I learned the truth, these incidents rose up in memory abstracted to essentials, like line drawings—a stick man in the circle of a float tube drifting hopefully over an empty, transparent plane; a cartoon figure blithely floating flies on a lifeless band of effluent streaming from a chemical tank hidden behind him. What exactly did it mean that I could spend hours at this and never suspect? That the center was gone and I couldn't even tell?

In the strange circularity of experience, this is in a way how it all began, not how I started fishing, but how I started believing in it. At the customary age for such things, I was enrolled in a parochial grade school, and within two years suffered what is known as a "crisis of faith," though it seemed to me then, as it does now, a crisis of reason. If Adam and Eve were the first people, I wondered, then who was there in Eden to draw the picture of the unfortunate pair (indisputably reproduced in my cate-chism for all to see) weeping beneath a giant hand that sternly pointed to the exit? And among all the beasts rubbernecking the world's first evic-tion, where, I demanded to know, was *Tyrannosaurus rex*? Such are the questions that hound the mind of an eight-year-old literalist, and I was duly referred to the proper ecclesiastical authorities. There was much talk, through which drifted the vapors of canonical incense. I smelled only smoke.

In the usual fashion, I put misgiving to the test, looked for signs and found only disillusionment. Finally I decided, though I didn't express it this way at the time, that you could put your faith in a cosmic beard, or you could put your faith in other things; all had about the same capacity to please or disappoint. It was just harder to blame the other things for their imperfections. From then on, I took my metaphysics on pretty much an ad hoc basis. If one had to be anchored to something, which ap-peared beyond question, it might as well be fishing, which seemed then as it does now among the least cynical of all human occupations. And next to all the weeping statues, all the visages of saints miraculously im-printed on tortillas, next to the Simjase Silver Star Center founded on the Twelve Bids of Patule revealed to Edmund "Billy" Meier by extraterres-trial Space Brothers—next to these, fishing looks pretty reasonable.

Time has tempered these views somewhat and taken them the long way around, perhaps inevitably, to a vision of things in season. And one of these seasonal things is the vision itself. It's a now-you-see-it, now-you-don't world, that spins in a circle of ongoing renegotiation. And this, it seems to me, is the essence of comedy, though perhaps not itself essen-tially comic.

Certainty becomes doubt, and the skeptic, questioning a faith in his own incapacity to know, believes again.

An exhausted fox curls into a ball and wakes up as a hedgehog who, after a time, adopts foxy ways.

A hobbling fisherman loses his limp and rights himself on pink toes of ordinary size, with all his hair settling back onto what you might call his 'ed.

And the summer wheels on.

11

<hr>

Everything That Rises, Everything That Flies

<hr>

The glassy grain of water looking upward I see the bed

Of the river above me upside down very clear

What am I doing here in mid-air?

—Ted Hughes, "Wadwo"

. . . knowing he has been struck

by what rises from under the surface

like the very first dream of morning.

—Robert Siegel, "The Very First Dream of Morning"

1.

Everywhere, the world is pattern—the hexagonal replication of snow-flakes and honeycomb, the linear striations of rocks, the concentric rip-ples of a rise. The geometries of motion are likewise symmetrical, and in season, great migratory waves advance and retreat like tides. Whales ply the Pacific from Baja to Alaska; oak savannahs encroach on the prairie in wet years and are driven back in droughts; strings of geese traverse the hemisphere, always a wingbeat to the south of Arctic air; a hundred million hooves pound circles round the Serengeti. Incessant currents of species run circuits on a world that itself orbits, spins, and precesses, and the earth becomes a fractal of motion.

Human beings answer the echoes of their own migratory imperatives. Sun-seeking wealth Airstreams to Phoenix on the first cold winds of November. Under the vernal equinox, schools of spawning collegians, ripe with hormones and beer, wash up like grunion on the beaches of Fort Lauderdale. And beneath a broiling August sun, the concrete-dwellers of Detroit, Chicago, and Minneapolis journey to cool woods and glacial lakes nearer the Canadian border.

This last was the pattern of my youth, a regional pilgrimage that I incorporated into my own cycles of migration. It was a much-anticipated exodus to the Promised Land, an annual rediscovery of Eden before the fall where immense prehistoric pike lurked in weedbeds and innocent panfish could be caught by the hundreds. Such places were located in the upper reaches of Michigan, Wisconsin, and Minnesota, though the Midwestern vernacular dispensed with such technicalities, subsuming them all in the sweeping locution, "up north." For a few weeks each summer, everyone went up north and if the designation was geographically nonspecific, it nonetheless called to mind the same clear picture for all—deep, crystalline, birch-fringed lakes; stands of white pine; tamarack swamps; cranberry bogs; whitetailed deer and garbage bears. Though hardly wild country, it performed for me the same mental offices as wilderness, and for much of my life, "north" was the direction of primal places, of aboriginal promise, and most of all, of rivers cold enough to grow trout. The farther north, the better the fishing. Latitude was everything.

The landscape of the West, however, has since raised my fishing into three dimensions. Where once there were only the rolling prairies and the level woodlands of glacial sand-country, there are now magnificent peaks, high meadows, thousands of square miles of mountains, and an entirely new direction. I no longer migrate "up north." I simply go "up."

As simple facts sometimes do, the discovery of altitude represented a paradigmatic shift in thinking. Old notions about where to travel to find trout streams became useless in a geography where latitude was a matter of almost complete indifference. One could travel east, or west, or strangest of all, even south to find fishing. Maps no longer expressed simple and predictable gradients of temperature, planar surfaces with a magic line, above which the fishing began. Compass needles were no longer magnetized to point automatically at trout. The new landscape was a geometric solid that projected upward into vertical strata of climate, through successive zones of rainfall, temperature, and ecological variety. I found myself at the bottom of a sedimentary atmosphere, and the matter of finding fish no longer hinged on the tools of the cartographer but of the archaeologist.

Even then, there were adjustments to make. The world was backward, or rather, upside down. The archaeologist excavates a hole in the past and unearths centuries by the shovelful, descending through consecutive layers of origin—of human life, of mammals, of flowering plants, vertebrates, fishes, of insects, microbes, and primal sludge. Life stacks up and its beginnings are down. But a fisherman ascends through time; the origins he seeks are the newest things rather than the oldest. A trout stream begins in the slow seep of mountain snowmelt or the shallow trickle at the outlet of a high-elevation lake. The farther you rise, the closer you come to the sources; the highest streams are the youngest and freshest. The archaeologist and the angler, though, have at least this in common—if they go far enough, both will strike water.

There is a paradox to altitude: Traveling toward these origins of newness seems to push time backward. The direction is antihistorical, to destinations that have been least touched by the years and remain most like what they once were. Embracing a time when the world was young, mountain places seem ancient, in just the way that memories of childhood seem at once old and new, remote from the present but summoning a time when life was fresh to you, and you to it. "Up" is the direction of the primeval and wild that seems age-old and just born. Even the season expresses the paradox. As the year spirals upward into the thinner, cooler atmosphere of autumn, summer lags here, and wildflowers long dried to husky seed pods in the valley are just beginning to bloom in the mountains. A passing summer like an ocean-bound trout stream is reborn at high elevation and will remain, for a few weeks yet, a promise fulfilling itself. Perched on the cusp of summer and fall, it is the highest vantage point of the year.

This elevation brings with it a sense of stored power. As you rise with the mountains, each increment of altitude measures a gain in a kind of latent force. We are apt to equate energy with kinesis, with mass in motion, but there is as well a hidden power in stasis, a potential energy that a body possesses solely by virtue of its position. An energy of the possible lies dormant in a boulder on the summit merely because it *could* be rolling down the mountainside. Within things lurks a coiled dynamic that owes its existence to gravity, at once the most ordinary and mysterious of all forces. That two bodies should exert an attraction and be drawn together for no other reason than that they are both material is one of the strangest circumstances in the universe. We appear to share something intrinsic with both hydrogen atoms and galaxies. In hiking up a high-altitude stream, the accumulating potential energy is both a physically felt intensity and a rising potency of spirit, and both are powered by gravity, which is the force that holds the universe together and, by no coincidence, what makes rivers run in the first place.

So I gravitate to the high ground and its sense of potential and newness within age, and drive three hundred miles to the Blue Mountains and the small headwater streams of the John Day, the Malheur, and Grande Ronde watersheds. The Blues lie bunched together in steep, carved ridges crowded into the northeast corner of the state. To the north, they slope down to high-desert flats that slip quietly into the Columbia River. To the east, the mountains drop abruptly into the deepest river gorge on the continent, 6,000 feet down to the bottom of Hell's Canyon of the Snake River. On the western and southern flanks, they are surrounded by open, arid rangeland. Bounded like this on all sides, the Blue Mountains rise like an island of altitude from the land around them.

This was not always the case. Two hundred million years ago, much of the Pacific Northwest was simply the Pacific, lying as yet unborn on the continental shelf under hundreds of fathoms of ocean whose surf pounded the base of the Blues. They were then part of the original coastal range, born of a geological restlessness that would last 150 million years.

North America rests on a sixty-mile-thick chunk of the earth's crust; the floor of the Pacific forms another such plate of rock, and the two drift freely, if slowly, over the hot, pliable core of the planet. Oregon was born in the clash of these gigantic plates. It was more of a glancing blow than a head-on collision, as the heavier plate of the ocean bottom slid beneath the continental crust. The passage was not a smooth one. The western edge of North America gouged the surface of the Pacific floor as it passed beneath, scraping up enormous volumes of mud, sediment, and sand that piled up and jammed together against the edge of the continent and slowly formed a chain of mountains along the coast. The Blues were among the first of these, but the process continued; new mountains were formed to the west of the older ones, which weathered and eroded and were sometimes awash in the basalt flows of unremitting volcanic activity inland. The Northwest literally rose from the sea, and as more land grew to the west, the Blue Mountains, in a sense, migrated to the east, to where they now stand hundreds of miles from the ocean, one of the oldest parts of the region.

I first catch sight of the Blues indirectly. Having driven for hours through parched, treeless sagebrush range, I at last turn north and within minutes meet a dozen oncoming trucks stacked with lodgepole and Ponderosa logs, wrestled from the mountains and headed to a mill. That a forest should exist somewhere in this landscape seems inconceivable. Even from the tops of rises on the highway, I see no trees anywhere on the long, receding vistas. The road drops into a shallow canyon, and in half-an-hour, I'm suddenly in the middle of it, climbing steep grades of switchbacks and evergreens.

Cresting the last ridge, one eye on the road and the other on the dashboard and an increasingly restless temperature gauge, I coast into the Logan Valley, a broad, stunningly beautiful mile-high meadow at the foot of the Strawberry Mountains. An open expanse of summer-green grasses and wildflowers, rimmed with lodgepole, it looks like Yellowstone. Half-a-dozen tiny creeks crisscross the valley, and where one of them runs beneath the road, I pull over to let the truck cool. Something beneath the hood emits a steamy belch and hisses in the stillness.

The stream is even smaller than it first appeared. I could jump across it almost anywhere, and the smooth sheet of water is so clear and shallow as to be nearly invisible over the tawny bottom of sand and gravel. There doesn't look like enough water to hold trout, but from a habit I've never been able to break, I scrounge the roadside grasses for insects and turn up an immature grasshopper and a couple of ladybugs. Dropped into a little pool below the corrugated-steel highway culvert, they wash downstream. I track them until they disappear into the glare. I watch a moment longer and am turning to leave, when fifty feet down the creek, the surface is broken by the faintest of rises radiating softly from the bankside grasses. A rising trout—of any size—is the most powerful inducement in fly fishing, and I briefly weigh the prospect of breaking out my stuff and rigging up for the sole purpose of taking half-a-dozen casts at a trout that might push four inches. It's a tight call. In the end I decide against it, preemptively embarrassed by the ridiculous spectacle I might present to a passing car—a grown man in a thousand dollars worth of equipment, kneeling in head-high grass, fishing intently to no more water than trickles through an average suburban gutter after a light rain. Although I don't mind being thought a fool, I do hesitate going out of my way to manufacture an occasion for it. Still, one can't dismiss the omen. Reluctant to abandon the little stream altogether, I fill an empty beer can with icy creek water and drain it into the radiator.

Across the valley, the highway rises and winds to 6,000 feet. A rough logging road cuts south and, ten miles farther in, skirts the edge of a narrow meadow and the headwaters of the North Fork of the Malheur River, where I will spend the next few days. The upper river flows in and out of many such meadows in the woods—some encompassing hundreds of acres, others no bigger than a church parking lot. The one I've come to is not large, perhaps a hundred and fifty hundred yards wide and four times that in length, little more than a hesitation in the immense tract of mixed conifer forest. The meadow is completely enclosed by lodgepole pine, thick Ponderosas, a few species of fir, here and there a spruce, and at the boggy margin of the clearing, old and nearly limbless tamaracks. Their perfectly straight, massive, tapering trunks spear a small cone of branches, bearing delicate green needles so small and sparse they seem incapable of sustaining an organism of such size, like a sixty-ton whale that feeds exclusively on plankton. Such whales once swam in sight of the Blues, and the mountains have kept the disproportion of their existence alive in the tamaracks. The woods have not been left untouched, though, logged some time in the years before I was born. But by some benign accident, a great many of the large trees survived, and if the place isn't truly primeval, there is still a powerful feeling of primalness about it.

The meadow must have proven too remote and too wet to till and too small to graze, shielded by insignificance from the mechanisms that would turn it into money. I imagine that the clearing is much as it has always been. Along one edge of the meadow flows the "river," a small, cobbled creek on a gradient gentle enough to encourage a wide meander. Like the tamaracks, the stream is sustained by tiny things, fed by imperceptible seeps scattered about the meadow that keep the ground spongy enough to prevent trees from taking solid root. In dry years, fire keeps the meadow open and renews its dense profusion of grasses and wildflowers—two varieties of paintbrush, a pale lily with a throat speckled scarlet as a fever, fireweed and skyrocket, gentian, the lush telescoping stalks of corn lily, and an astonishing number of bog candles, an orchid that sprouts a succulent, jadelike shoot two-feet tall and covered with tiny white blooms. Waterhemlock and brookline fringe the stream, and in a few silted oxbows, ranunculus sends up strawberry-like blossoms.

These meadows in the mountains are to me among the most intimate of all landscapes, intensely personal spaces removed from the world below. The treeline is pushed back just far enough to offer the reassurance of openness, but is still sufficiently close by to give a sense of location in the landscape. In such clearings you inhabit a world with surveyable bounds, and so one that appeals to a deep animal propensity for frequenting the edges of things. The pastoral nestles within the wild in a confluence of opposites that is both serene and energizing.

The fish are proportioned to the place, small wild rainbows that rise without suspicion to almost anything, and for days I fish an Elk Hair Caddis almost exclusively, a fly so buoyant and visible that simply watching the drift is its own pleasure. The trout lie exactly in trouty spots, in troughs along the bank, in the deeper water (which is never very deep) against bends, in pools scoured in the gravel, below the crown of a fallen tree that trails in the water. The trout respond in pleasant synchrony with your efforts, coming more frequently as you cast with greater care and place your fly a few critical inches closer to their lies, striking less often when your attention is captured by the landscape and you fish more casually.

Some trout are smaller, others a little larger; all finally are of modest size, and that too is one of the delights of the place. Like any angler, I am fascinated by big fish, by their comparative scarcity and the difficulty of catching them. Yet there is a disturbing compulsion in fly fishing, particularly these days, to regard the largest trout as always the best. A brand of gunnysack-ism persists in the era of catch-and-release, and you feel the weight of an unspoken assumption: that the way, the proper way, to go about fishing is to seek out the best water and do what's necessary to extract its trophies. Anything less makes you less than a serious fisherman, a lightweight if you don't succeed, a mere dabbler if you don't care to try— angling's version of the "be all you can be" mentality that insists upon its own somewhat diminished notion of being. But the attitude is pervasive, relentlessly vended in magazines and books and fly shops, where the only trout worth mentioning run so many inches or pounds, and the failure to catch them is attended by the subtle guilt that you're not "doing your best." Worse, this disposition has ruined (my term, not theirs) some fine fishermen for whom the progress of fly fishing has become only an escalation in the size of the catch. After a week or two hooking salmon nonstop in Alaska or boating giant rainbows below Lee's Ferry, they no longer find pleasure in home waters; they fish for smaller trout, if they fish them at all, with a certain despondency, ruefully calculating how many of them it would take to make a Costa Rican tarpon or sea-run brown in Tierra del Fuego. Each seven-inch trout becomes a measurement of lack. The fish of a lifetime can make your day and spoil something larger. But these headwaters have no subcurrent of compulsion. Each rise is a small thrill, prompting no disappointment that it somehow could have been more.

Still, nothing cuts more deeply against the psychological grain of fly fishing than complete predictability. The essence of a trout stream lies partly in its capacity for surprise, and fishing a dry fly to a little bankside run off the main channel, I catch a velvety ten-inch bull trout—a species neither common, nor commonly caught on the surface. This single fish is exactly the kind of rarity that gives texture to a trip.

The very boundedness of the meadow and the tangibility of its limits curls your awareness inward, creating a small enclosed world inside of which boundaries disappear. There ceases to be much difference between fishing for trout, watching birds through binoculars, exploring the meadow, boiling creek water for coffee, waiting for the deer that will browse at dusk on the fringe of the clearing—all of these flow together as contiguous, borderless events and become the simple, indivisible current of being there. Big rivers and their big fish impress themselves most as a magnificence and power, but these small places are for me the archetype of fly fishing, which also dissolves the borders between things. To fish the fly is very much an involuted occupation, folding and refolding in successive layers of detail that surround some central core, and though no one can speak with certainty about the origin of fly fishing, I think it could only have begun in a landscape as intimate and interior as this one.

After three days of fishing the meadow up and down, many times over, I begin to feel the pull of other waters, and eventually head farther into the Blue Mountains. Past Elk Flats the road ascends to a pass near Baldy Mountain, a bare pate with a shaggy fringe like an old man's head. I pull over at the summit, a point of potential that is the privilege of altitude. To the south lies the Malheur; to the east, the headwaters of the Burnt River; opposite those, the beginnings of the John Day; and a few miles to the north, the first trickles of the first streams that will become the Grande Ronde. They converge at this elevation like some reclaimed instant of the past when what lay ahead was all possibility, each watershed a still-secret future cutting an unseen path through the mountains with its own inevitable gravity. I go north.

On the way, I detour to Prairie City, to stop first at a service station and then the Forest Service office. To go deeper into the Blues, I'll need more fuel and better maps.

On the way back from the valley, I pass a scattering of tents pitched along the stream. None are the trim, rip-stop, and shock-corded rigs of weekend campers; they are old, unwieldy sheets of faded canvas stretched over wooden poles and sisal guys. I see perhaps a dozen sites in a three-mile stretch, every one a little different, all essentially the same: tent, clothesline, a few chairs, a lantern hung on a tree stob, sometimes a card table, firepit and stacked splits, three or four coolers in a shady spot, a dusty pickup. The ground around them is trampled to bare dirt by the caulk boots of loggers, working a show too far from home to make the daily round-trip an option. So they set up camp. Sometimes, they drive home for the weekends; more often, wives and kids shuttle up with supplies, clean laundry, and a little company for husbands who've staked out a temporary home as they pass through the summer season of work.

An hour farther in, there's evidence of other migrations. At a tiny spring where I stop for lunch and a beer, elk sign is everywhere. I follow a game trail leading into the hills, up to the high valleys and late-summer range, but the woods are too dry to walk quietly, and I spook only a pair of blue grouse that fly a few feet to a deadfall, and look at me stupidly.

Not many miles distant, another trail passes near here, a thin trickle of hope, discontent, and desperation that led west in the last century. I imagine that some migrants on the Oregon Trail, with beasts, baggage, and spirits much diminished by the long trip through the Rockies, probably saw the elephant somewhere around here, and could or would go no farther. They settled in the valleys and draws, casting their lot with the mountains. When the first shell exploded over Fort Sumter, another, more deliberate migration followed in their path, destined for the Blue Mountains and energized by the most magnetic of minerals: gold.

All the Hollywood and history-book bilge about wide-open spaces, the spirit of the frontier, manifest destiny, and the advance of democratic values—all that notwithstanding, the opening of the West was first and foremost the biggest get-rich-quick scheme in the chronicle of America. Though we tend to think of that era of settlement as a movement of the East to the West, it is equally true that the West went East—in ships loaded with Port Orford cedar, in great bundles of pelts, on the hooves of cattle, and in bars of gold and silver. If civilization eventually took hold of the West, its chief and most enduring value was "take the money and run."

The discovery of gold in the Blues spread eastward as well, a venture with all the dynamics of its modern counterpart, the chain letter. The first arrivals milked the mountains and skimmed the cream, working the placer deposits, panning or sluicing the alluvial rubble for particles of gold that had eroded from the mountains. The ones who came later found only the arduous and unremunerative toil of mining the deep stream gravels and primary ores in the bedrock. There was no mother-lode here. The veins were thin, irregular, difficult. By the time Lincoln was assassinated, most of the miners, like most of the easy gold, were gone, moved farther east toward Hell's Canyon, where richer deposits were discovered. Every nook and crevice of the mountains swelled, for a few seasons, with exuberant hope that drained away leaving only disap-pointment and ghost towns—Cornucopia, Copperfield, Homestead.

But hope, unlike gold, springs eternal, and in this century, the hopeful have returned, though their numbers are fewer. Driving up re-mote streams like Clear Creek or Granite Creek, you pass a weird world that peels back layers of time. Bigger, more modern operations work the lower stretches with bulldozers and dredges, excreting enormous waste piles of smooth, beautiful riverstone. Farther on, less sophisticated setups get by with homebuilt wooden sluices, rickety water diversions, and the occasional Bobcat. Higher still in the headwaters are the most primitive sites, with shovels and pans. Every claim is staked with a sign: "Eldora-do—Keith Buckrum," "Empty Pan—Jay and Jean McNichols—Keep Out Anyway," "The Gulches—Est. 1950—No Trespassing." But even the crudest sites are tempered by anachronisms. A grubby little claim is overlooked by a brand new prefab log house; another is flanked by a big Airstream trailer, the side ripped off to make an equipment shed, the hulk held on the slope with logging chains anchored to deadmen buried deep in the hillside; farther up a sieve-like board shack propped with two-by-twelves has an immaculate Mercedes parked in front; a decaying lean-to shades a campstove and a shiny black Barcalounger. Everywhere, there are enough raccoon-nibbled garbage bags and rusting piles of crap to sap whatever small romance may linger in the scene. But old urges persist and from the latecoming spring to the early-arriving fall, hopeful souls still return to hunt for the big one.

I hunt too, and in similar places. High in the headwaters above 6,000 feet, I prospect riffles and alluvial fans of tiny pools with a dry fly.

There are no pots of gold, but plenty of rainbows, or so they seem at first. I catch four or five of them before realizing that these small, silvery, bullet-shaped fish, perfectly uniform in size, are not residents, but migrants—the smolts of wild steelhead spawned at these altitudes to spend a season before returning to the ocean. Their presence here collapses millennia. Anadromous salmonids evolved when the Blues were nearer the Pacific, and as land rose to the west and the mountains inched eastward, the steelhead followed, returning season after season, each migration a little longer and a little more difficult. And now they navigate seven hundred circuitous miles, 6,000 feet of altitude, and a hundred million years to this spot at the heart of the heart of the mountains, surfacing high in this oldest of places. Altitude is a fortification, and it is also fortifying. The steelhead accumulate the energy of elevation and deposit its potential in eggs amid the stream gravel. In Greek, "anadromous" means "running upward," and the fish, like the fisherman, rise to sources, reimplanting an original idea and reclaiming a world perpetually young.

The smolts are a dizzying continuity—not merely of seasonal recurrence, or of species, but a continuity of saline oceans and springwater creeks, of pelagic valleys and inland mountaintops, of origins and eventualities. And these are best discovered from a vantage point with a little elevation.

2.

I am not surprised that so many fly fishermen develop a strong and abiding fascination with birds—watching and identifying them, learning their habits and seasons, tying flies with their plumage. Certainly, wandering around on rivers gives ample opportunity for these things, and to some degree the interest in birds is a particular dimension of a more comprehensive involvement with the world that borders a trout stream. But this doesn't explain it all. Creatures that impinge more directly on the life and affairs of fish—otters and seals, algae and mircroorganisms—elicit by comparison only passing attention. They are curiosities. With birds, something more intrinsic seems at stake.

A clue to what that might be comes to me on this headwater creek, as I crawl up a flat shingle of bedrock that angles over the only pool I've seen that could conceivably be called "large." Looking down from the edge, I glimpse briefly, out of the corner of my eye, a dark form beneath the surface. It darts quickly ahead and vanishes into the shaded water at the throat of the pool. I do what any fisherman would, reacting in two completely opposite ways. First, through a pair of polarized sunglasses, I scan the pool for any sign of a fish that I may have spooked. Then, finding nothing, I look up through the jagged, stream-shaped breach in the canopy and search the sky for a passing hawk, or vulture, or eagle that may have cast a quick shadow on the pool. Nothing there either. Whether the gliding image was fish or fowl, though, seems less significant to me than the fact that I can't make the determination, that two so apparently different sources failed to register their difference. The fleeting shadow below—an early returning steelhead? some restless bird pushing out on the near edge of autumn?—flickers over the mind and hints at disparities only seeming, at some essential unity of things that rise and things that fly.

I once saw a photograph of a large wall mural painted by artist Bill Reid. The figure is that of a chum salmon, rendered in a fashion both anatomically accurate and stylistically consistent with an old Haida tradition of totemic images. Like the Paleolithic paintings of bison in the Lascaux caves, ancient Egyptian carvings of birds, and Australian petroglyphs, this salmon represents both the animal and a deeply felt idea about the animal. Contained within the body of the salmon, continuous with its outline, are the images of birds, stylized suggestions but unmistakably avian—the long hooked bills of eagles, gulls, and cormorants; the dark eyes of ravens. Fish and birds cohere in a single, unified, interlocking form, the quietly powerful emblem of a fundamental unity once known, now forgotten or never learned. For some reason, this is called "primitivism."

Any fisherman who keeps his eyes open can't help but see these same connections implied almost everywhere. In the halcyon days of June, deep in a mountain cleft, a knobby and neckless kingfisher squats in an alder snag above a bedrock pool. It rolls forward, cups its wings at the last instant, and plunges down to spear its own reflection in the water, transforming it into a silver salmon smolt squirming in a thick bill. A hundred luckier fish scatter in panic, an explosion of tiny glints fleeing the point of impact like a pane of shattered glass. They dart in confusion beneath the blue water, a randomness of quick shimmers that brings to mind a flock of songbirds I once watched. They were driving off a crow, diving and mobbing it, flashing like sparks when they turned broadside to the sun, then suddenly wheeling into invisibility and rematerializing somewhere else. The flock blinked on and off like a swarm of minnows, and its general movement could be tracked only by the steady retreat of the crow.

A fisherman does well to heed the creatures that fly. Up a coastal headwater, I followed a green heron, a secretive bird that was long ago called a "fly-up-the-creek." It moved slowly upstream, smoothly and quietly from pool to pool, fishing the places I would fish and approaching them as I would.

On the coast, herring gulls and brown pelicans work schools of baitfish driven to the surface, trying to escape the frenzied attacks of larger fish beneath them. On a trout stream, swallows sense the hatch before it happens and circle above the river in anticipation. They skim the surface when insects appear and leave rings like riseforms. Twice, swallows have plucked my dry fly from the water, carrying the line aloft and pulsing exactly like trout. "You always see birds first," writes Nick Lyons. "On rivers, on saltwater, they are the great harbingers of fish feeding." For the fisherman, birds still reenact their ancient role of augury.

Standing on a bridge one midsummer day, years and miles from here, I leaned over the rail and stared into the waters of a little spring creek, cress-lined and bright as a diamond, with a dozen varieties of aquatic plants in a patchwork of violent-greens. A trout rose. Then again. Watching the still radiating rise, I saw a small brown trout sidle out of the cress to sip a third, pale mayfly. Shortly, more fish began working the edge of the weeds and more flies emerged, some lifting from the surface and rising vertically past the bridge rail in front of me. From the bankside elms and oaks, a cedar waxwing appeared on an easy bobbing float and snatched a mayfly almost in front of my nose. It plucked the fly with the same audible snap and the same tight swirling turn that a trout makes, and disappeared back to the leafy cover. More birds followed, and soon seven or eight waxwings were gliding in alternation from the trees, working the hatch over the water while an equal number of trout edged out of the watercress to do the same. Leaning over the rail, I saw the bridge, myself, birds and trout, mirrored in a glassy surface and showing a small patch of world for a moment in perfect parallel.

It is this about birds, I think, that registers so powerfully on a fisherman and is sensed by him as somehow familiar. Like fish, birds inhabit a forbidden atmosphere of transparent velocities, pressure envelopes and gradients, fluid vectors, downdrafts and upwellings. Between hydrodynamics and aerodynamics, there is only a difference in density, not kind. Birds and fish move effortlessly in fully dimensioned worlds with three degrees of freedom, almost heedless of gravity. Above and below the plane of the earth they hint at the geometric thinness of terrestrial existence and the attractions of depth and altitude.

A blue heron knifes its bill underwater to seize a fish; a trout pokes its nose in the air for drifting insects. Water ouzels literally fly underwater; salmon leap to swim through the air over whitewater rapids. At the surface of the water, birds shade into fish, and overlapping scales are layered into feathers, like the transmutations of an Escher drawing. The earth may spin on a polar axle, but for the fisherman, the horizon is its axis of symmetry. Where atmospheres meet—on a mountain lake or saltwater flat—birds swim through an aqua sky and fish fly in cerulean depths.

3.

For a fisherman, this idea of the surface inevitably rises to the top, and there's little wonder why this should be so. Fly fishing is a matter of faith, and like all faiths, it contains a central miracle: the rise of a trout to a dry fly.

In his *Physics*, Aristotle explains what he sees as the governing principle of nature—all things seek their origins. Human beings are held to the ground and prevented from flying off into the air because the body is composed of soil and so clings to the earth by virtue of this affinity. By the same logic, the spirit of a man is of heavenly origin and eventually seeks its celestial home. For Aristotle, the soul tends upward; spiritual things naturally rise. This is the only proposition I know of that broaches a metaphysical argument for dry-fly fishing.

The floating fly seems the very thing for which fly fishing was designed. But in fact, intentionally dressing flies for buoyancy and fishing in a manner to keep them afloat are comparatively new innovations. As a deliberate technique, widely practiced, dry-fly fishing is perhaps only a century or so old. Since then, it has transformed the sport. If fly fishing was not invented for the dry fly, it was reinvented for it, and surface fishing has come to transcend all other approaches in the angling imagination.

That this recent notion has substantially reorganized our thinking about such an old occupation is in itself highly suggestive, particularly since dry-fly fishing, when gauged against the ordinary criteria, generally proves an unremarkable method. Under most circumstances, it is demonstrably not the best way to take fish, especially large ones. It is not the simplest technique—that honor probably goes to the wet fly. Nor is it the most difficult; nymph fishing, done properly, demands more intense concentration, more exacting line control, a keener eye, and quicker reflexes.

Nonetheless, the floating fly draws fishermen with an ineluctable gravity, and the source of this attraction is not difficult to locate. It originates in a flash, in the abrupt and certain take of a trout. Few moments in fishing hold the same immediacy and vividness as the rise to a floating fly, and none are endowed with the same satisfying sense of closure. In an instant, the take creates dry-fly fishing, separating it from all other techniques, and defining its most compelling attraction.

Dry-fly fishing emerges on the far side of "what happens" and fixes itself on the idea of "where," on the focal plane of the surface. Here, the symmetrical domains of air and water converge to form both a mirror and a barrier. And I think that the fascination of the dry fly arises from this paradoxical character of the surface, at once hinting richly at the life below, while obscuring our apprehension of it.

This capacity to reveal and conceal simultaneously is most apparent in the visual sense. The swells, slicks, roils, and riffles answer to the workings of deeper currents and streamed topographies, tracing, if imperfectly, the hidden contours of the river. Yet at the same time the fluctuating and reflective surface inhibits our ability to see beneath it.

The particular nature of this restriction is significant, for we are overwhelmingly visual creatures—in both the way we describe and operate in our world, and, more importantly, the way we know it. Our discourse abounds in words and expressions that equate vision with understanding: "I see" denotes recognition and comprehension; to "shed some light on the subject" metaphorically unites the perception of the eye with that of the mind; to put something "in perspective" suggests an intellectual ordering that derives from visual, spatial relationships. "To be enlightened," "to bring something out in the open," "to make it clear" (or "to remain in the dark")—in a hundred such usages we equate our capacity to know with our capacity to see. And the same equation lies at the heart of angling's most telling phrase, "reading the water," which links a visual process with an analytical one.

Riding on the surface, a dry fly becomes a point of contact between the world of the fisherman and that of the fish, the nexus of eye and mind. It is the visual extension of our imagination, probing what can't be seen and charting the shape of human inquisitiveness and expectancy. A drifting fly is a test, a series of questions inscribed on the surface: "Are the trout here?" "Have I alarmed them?" "Does the fly pattern adequately resemble something that belongs in this place?"—in short, "Have I accurately inferred and observed the principles by which the river works?"

At the instant of the take, the boundary of the surface is shattered. Hidden things are disclosed. We have tempted a separate world to reveal itself to us, to our eyes and imaginations. The take is the visual analog of an answered question, a curiosity satisfied, the visible confirmation that we have, if only locally and temporarily, understood some small thing about a river: the dynamics of its atmosphere; the habits of its trout; their mechanisms of predation; the character of their instincts. The take transports us, imaginatively, from one domain to another. And although human characteristics are commonly ascribed to fish behavior—"curiosity," "playfulness," "rage"—in fact, quite the opposite is true. When a fish takes a fly, it hasn't become more manlike; rather, the angler has become more fishlike. Each cast tries the limits of the river; each take successfully integrates us into its processes and offers an increment of understanding.

Much of fishing is a physical experience, an electric and buoyant thrill like bubbles in the blood. But the take is a subtler affair that appeals to the intellect and awareness. For even the surface itself, the boundary we fish on, is itself an imaginative construct. In reality, only the water and air exist; the interface between them—some third, separate place we call the "surface"—is something we create. Our brains are not wired to accept the deep anarchy of absolute disjunction, and so we invent thresholds and zones of transition that soothe our understanding with little continuities and make us feel better. The surface of the river is a hypothetical fulcrum, balancing the aquatic world with our own imperfect grasp of it. On this plane of our own invention, we cast our surmise, wonder, and hope bound up in so much feather and fur.

The take instantaneously validates our efforts, conferring a measure of definitiveness and closure to an enterprise otherwise riddled with uncertainty and inconclusiveness. Few things in life, I think, have this to offer. A rising trout is an upward-tending thing, and the surface of a river is the ceiling of its world with all the clarifying power of altitude.

4.

The last of summer dissipates against the surface of autumn, and in a migration with its own symmetry, I leave the Blue Mountains in the extreme northeast for the Klamaths in the very southwest. The geographical distance is bridged by an ancient connection—two hundred million years ago, the Blues adjoined the Klamaths, and the Klamaths the Sierra Nevada, forming a single contiguous chain of Pacific coastal mountains. It now takes a full day of hard driving to reestablish the link.

But I'm drawn here as much by discontinuity, by the peculiar character of the Klamaths that was forged a hundred million years ago in a strange, almost anomalous geological event. For reasons not clearly understood, the Klamaths broke away from the coastal chain and moved sixty miles out into the ocean, creating an island that would not reconnect to the mainland for fifty million years. It was insulated from the almost ceaseless volcanic activity on the edge of the continent by a shallow strait sixty miles wide, and when the strait eventually filled in to form the dry land, the world around the Klamaths was an entirely different place.

Landlocked again, the Klamaths still retain some of their insular character—distinct from the newer coastal mountains to the north; separated from the Blues by the recently formed Cascades and the broad basalt flows of central Oregon; the ancient link with the Sierras now overlaid by the wide volcanic Modoc Plateau. The Klamaths exist in a chaotic scramble of intercut and intruded rock. Mudstone, sandstone, shale, and basalt from the sea floor, serpentine and blueschist, gabbro, greenstone, granite, and andesite are heaved confusedly together by grinding tectonic pressure, and, in places, cooked by the heat of volcanoes. The oldest rocks in Oregon, dating back 425 million years, are found here.

Found here as well are remnants of the temperate forest that once stretched across the continent from Alaska to Greenland, and began retreating about the time the dinosaurs died out. In his absorbing study of the region, *The Klamath Knot*, David Raines Wallace tells of standing on a ridge in the Siskiyous and looking out in awe over "a community of trees at least forty million years old," the genetic precursor of modern conifer forests from Montana to New Mexico. The mountains, Wallace points out, contain "elements of flora and fauna that reach back farther into the past than any place west of the Mississippi River."

The Klamaths—the Kalmiopsis and Siskiyous in the north, the Salmon and Trinity Mountains in the south—are ancient and steady, but at the same time an anachronism and outpost. In my lifetime, the last living veteran of the Civil War died. I remember seeing a picture of him, his creased face and knobby hands, the last remnant of a formative episode of history who watched the world around him change into something else, until finally, like the Klamaths, he was an island of something old amid a landscape unfamiliarly new.

There is a curious reciprocity between people and landscapes. That human beings shape their immediate world, be it clearing the underbrush or draining a swamp or building a shopping mall, is easily and universally observable. The Klamaths have not escaped this entirely. The edges are being bitten away. On the coast, the last stands of Port Orford cedar and redwood are being hauled away in trucks. To the east, volcanically active zones are being explored as a source of energy, drilled by the same geothermal vampires that would happily suck Yellowstone cold and dry.

More subtle, though, is the way in which a landscape transforms its inhabitants, imbuing them with some share of its essence. The people of the Klamaths seem themselves set apart, self-contained. As in the Blues, there is mining here, but fewer of the big operations and fewer too of the dilettante-hobbyists who put in a few weekends a year just to say that they own a claim. The miners here are secretive and insular, lone hunters for gold haunting country not rich in it. A few, the most extreme, work the placers for platinum. Other of the Klamath residents would make the territory literally a world apart. Half in earnest, a perennial separatist movement rears its tiny head here and debates whether to sever ties with Oregon and California and declare a new state, or to secede from the union altogether. They do not like taxes. They look upon politicians as the most dangerous kind of fool. Like the mountains, they do not suffer fools.

Nothing grows old by being weak, and the power of the Klamaths is their power to absorb and transform. There was a fellow I knew briefly, who, between his love of fishing and a love affair with the bottle, pretty much ran his life to suit himself, when it wasn't the other way around. In this spirit, he built his own rods—idiosyncratic, mongrelized affairs that conformed to none of fishing's ordinary regularities. Choosing long, limber spinning-rod blanks, he wrapped thin wire to mount generic, midsized guides and fashioned untapered grips from rolled sheet-cork. The reel was attached with two hose clamps and allowed him to use the rod indiscriminately with casting, spinning, or fly tackle, as dictated by circumstance or whim. Some years back, he said, he'd had enough of where he'd been and where he was. He packed a little gear, a spare pair of hose clamps, and a Band-Aid box of sensimilla buds, and simply disappeared somewhere up in the Kalmiopsis. He came back a year later, he said, "different."

Altitude does peculiar things. In the Klamaths, where an old world is just born, the newness of antiquity transforms your sense of the possible. The forested peaks, the high meadows, the remote, shaded draws seem capable of concealing anything. Along Bluff Creek in the Siskiyous, a giant manlike footprint, sixteen inches long, was discovered, and if it was only the imprint of the immense psychic weight of this place, that is to me significant in itself. Countless tales of Bigfoot sightings circulate in this area; although I don't accept them as fact, I do take them as a kind of truth. Only an idea so large and so impossible is capable of containing the sense of potential that dwells in the landscape and of conveying the longing that it inspires. Whatever else the Bigfoot legends may represent, they speak to some desire to populate these elevations with an original version of ourselves, to include some primal humanity in the mystery of the place and so reclaim it. Not long ago I read a newspaper interview with an old logger who said that years back, working the woods as a young man, he'd seen one of the giant beasts. A few summers later, on the steep slopes near the Trinity River, an accident left him with a crushed knee and shattered tibia; since then, he'd been driving a pickup over remote logging roads, shuffling up the spurs on a bad leg, looking for tracks. He wanted to see a Bigfoot again before he died. I'd like to run into him while fishing up here, his story more interesting to me than the creature he pursues.

But high up, amid the fir and ferns and rocks of a mountain creek, I see no one. There are no meadows here. Through a narrow defile in the mountain slope, the water sculpts a bed among boulders, slabs of bedrock, and the rubble of erosion. Trees and brush crowd the banks and lace together overhead in a canopy above the water. With a short, light rod rigged for "tunnel fishing," wading in shorts and boots to make the climb easier, I bend low to work close-range sidearm casts. Even at midday, there's not much light in here. What sun does manage to filter through is reflected from the riffles in flickering wavelets against rock walls and a ceiling of needles and leaves. I work upstream in a strangely illuminated cave that twists to the heart of the mountain. The trout here, cutthroats, are not as numerous as the rainbows in the Malheur meadow, are smaller and warier, invisible in the broken water of small plunge pools and the dimness of stony troughs. And when they rise, they materialize from the river like flakes of current that suddenly cohere to grab a fly.

Wherever the water is deep, the trout are willing. Insects are sparse here, their hold made tenuous by the scouring spates of spring runoff and the lack of nutrients in the stream. Just a few miles away, the water filters out through mountain rock. Only once, in early afternoon, do I find stream insects in any numbers, though to call it a hatch would be stretching the matter. Over the course of fifteen minutes, I see perhaps twice that many mayflies, skating on a fan of current at the head of a pool, species unknown. Their enormous eyes are the color of polished bloodstone, bodies a faint mottling on scaly segmentations. They look like some tiny prehistoric lizard with wings, some terminal offshoot in the evolution of reptiles to birds—except that they are older than both and among the most ancient of insects. When dinosaurs browsed in tropical landscapes, mayflies had been hatching for a quarter of a billion years, long before there were trout. They are the first link in a chain that leads to this moment.

In the pool, three cutthroats rise eagerly at every opportunity, more aware than I am of how briefly it will last. As the last few flies drift down, I cast twice, catch two fish, and then move on.

In this steep terrain, the little stream doles itself out, one small piece at a time, unfolding in a succession of discrete scenes. Every angle in the creekbed, each climb to the next pool opens onto a fresh arrangement of rock, trees, sunlight and running water, as careless and careful as a Japanese painting. Each works an exclusive permutation on the raw materials of landscape, producing a singular beauty and framing the particulars by which it must be fished. Big waters hold the mystery of concealment and exercise an attraction by what lies unseen at the bottom. Small streams, their depths easily plumbed, hold the mystery of the next bend. The insistent curiosity to see one more pool, one more variation on a familiar theme, propels you upstream. Each new place resets the clock until suddenly you find yourself fishing at the far end of a day that has slid around you and left scarcely a trace of its passing. Somehow, it is always morning.

This is the gravity of primeval altitudes, where the potential for perceiving some original relation lives more easily in the thinner, clearer air, and peoples our imaginations with images commensurate with the shape of our wonder. In his dreams, an old logger walks the woods on young legs and watches a giant man/beast gliding among the trunks of forty-million-year-old firs. In mine, swallows skim transparent currents, and trout sip ancient mayflies that rise to a cobalt sky.

12

Harvests

The river is within us, the sea is all about us;

—T. S. Eliot, "The Dry Salvages"

Down to sea level, a precipitous drop from the mountains into the fall of the year.

We have been trained, particularly since Darwin, to envision the processes of nature as gradual, glacially incremental, measured in geological ticks. And more often than not, this accords with our limited perception of events, as we gauge them against the small yardsticks of our lives. But beneath the apparent seamlessness of slow change, we are learning of a nature that is sudden and cataclysmic, a universe of exploding supernovae, of prehistoric asteroidal collisions and volcanic detonations, of species transformed in a burst of evolutionary hiccups.

From time to time, this more elemental structure of change makes itself felt. Once each year, almost inadvertently, some elusiveness in the moment all at once becomes tangible—a particular quality of the light; an unexpected sharpness in a breeze; the rattle of a seedpod at the edge of awareness; the dry, husky smell of life evaporating. In some incidental event, you sense abruptly the first tinge of autumn. The recognition tips you over the fulcrum of seasons, and although more summery weather may come, it is no longer summer; a border has been crossed. And if you're a fisherman, you can't look at rivers in quite the same way after that. Every change is both an ending and a beginning, which makes them twice as inviting, and twice as hard, as anything else.

I rarely fish the coastal rivers in summer. I might, on occasion, hike the upper stretches to fish for wild cutthroats; less often, for the steelhead that summer there and stack up in the deeper places, monstrously out of proportion to the small headwater pools. I haven't been downstream, though, to the first dozen stream-miles above the head of tide, since March. In the long, rainless months, the water there warms and runs sluggishly; under the bright midyear sun, the fish are as little inclined to strike as I am to tempt them. Other rivers and other fish exert their pull. But in the first days of fall, I return to the lower river, to take stock of its waters in this season of reckonings.

Compared to autumn in the great hardwood forests of the East, fall in the coastal mountains is an apologetic, hangdog affair; at first I found it a great disappointment. The steady influence of marine air precludes the dry, sharp nights that produce the extravagant colors of dying. The few deciduous trees here, mostly alders and willows, retreat by inches into muddy yellows and unremarkable browns. Here and there, a few spindly maples make a stab at red but fail to pull it off with any authority. The firs stay as green as ever.

Instead, there is the gray color of dampness in long morning fogs that come with the cool ocean air, and this is the essence of autumn that I have since come to love. Mist shrouds these low mountains and amplifies their sense of remoteness. Slopes of Douglas fir, lapped in receding rows, fade dimly into invisibility, each more indistinct than the one before it, until the last finally merges into a solid bank of cloud that effaces any difference between land and sky. The effect is surreally three-dimensional, an infinite depth of field that is not a little forbidding. There is no discernible horizon, nothing to give perspective or closure to the landscape, nothing to locate yourself in relation to.

Here the deciduous trees are as inconsequential as their falling leaves. The foggy moisture is the first life of the season. It condenses on the needles of firs, pines, and cedars and replenishes thick mats of mosses that cling to the bark; their primitive efficiency in drawing sustenance from the heavy air scarcely requires the formality of soil. The moss is itself a medium for sprays of licorice fern that sprout twenty feet off the ground. Water dripped to the forest floor is soaked up by clubworts and more mosses, and regreens parched stands of swordfern that will grow six feet high by spring. Deadfall timber crumbles to a spongy punk in the humid air. A chainsaw left on the growing winter woodpile rusts overnight. And everywhere—everywhere—fungi come alive from long-dormant spores and mycelia. Not long ago, a researcher in the Upper Peninsula of Michigan discovered the largest and oldest living thing on the planet—a fungus, a single organism that extends over thirty-seven acres. It weighs a hundred tons and is thought to be ten thousand years old. The meek may indeed inherit the earth. I would not be at all surprised if a larger, more ancient organism were discovered in these mountains.

In a month or six weeks, the first heavy rains of autumn will wash a summer's worth of dust from the trees and debris from the banks. The river will swell with roily brown water flowing down to the ocean and with silvery salmon flowing up. Then, carloads of families with five-gallon buckets will take to the hills for chanterelles and king boletus, returning at dusk with loads of pale-gold and buckskin-colored wild mushrooms. Others will rake all day in the duff beneath the firs for a handful of marble-size truffles. But that comes later. Right now the season is just beginning; in clumps of tiny mushrooms, in small tiers of shelf fungi, in the slow crawl of threadlike tendrils that spread a net over the mountains, as the living reclaims the dead. What appears to be decay and decomposition is so only in the narrowest vision of things. This transformation and recirculation of nutrients is the foundation of life in the landscape, as it is the basis of life in other things. Bread, wine, cheese, and beer are all born of molds. The damp odors of loam, litter, and rich tidal mud downriver, drift with woodsmoke and smell like a beginning.

In the days when people kept track of such things, the full moon nearest the autumnal equinox was called the Harvest Moon, and the sea-run cutthroats that rode high tides up the estuary and into fresh water were called Harvest Trout, a ripening of the year and the first replenishing of life in the river. Now, the fish are more often called "bluebacks," an angler's term that rivals only "hellgrammite" in its inconsistency of regional usage and capacity for confusion. I much prefer "harvest trout," a name that accords so closely with their nature, but I am resigned to "blueback" for practical reasons.

Of anadromous fishes, the sea-run cutthroats are my favorite, and I have saved them for last. Salmon and steelhead, though I have fished them with eagerness and conviction at times, will always remain a little foreign to me, even as I come to know their home territory—and they mine. In this era of hatcheries, fish are transplanted as easily as people, and had I been born a decade later, the salmon and steelhead now in the Great Lakes might well have become as familiar to me as the brook and brown trout of inland waters.

It didn't happen that way. When I came West, I looked first for trout and discovered in the sea-run cutthroats the subtlest and best expression of the place, as indigenous to the Northwest rivers as the rivers are to the landscape. One of their deepest appeals is that bluebacks have, for the most part, remained wild things. Unlike salmon and steelhead, they have not fallen victim to "management," and have in fact endured by dint of their own apparent inconsequence—an accidental strategy but one of the few that seems destined to succeed in the late twentieth century. They represent, in a sense, survival by negation. They don't grow very large; they don't occur in colossal numbers; they aren't as predictable as other anadromous fish; and they don't run in dense, heavy schools. Such circumstances hold little of interest for most fishermen, either commercial or sport, who have fixed their eyes on bigger game and better odds. Simple neglect has spared the blueback from the fate of becoming a market commodity, of the kind sold in cans or the variety hawked in the lascivious centerfolds of outdoor magazines.

Economically valueless and recreationally insignificant, the sea-run cutthroat has similarly furnished little incentive for study by university biologists and wildlife managers; as a result, we haven't learned quite enough about these fish to screw them up. Yet. But all that is gold does not glitter, and harvest trout remain one of the innermost secrets of the river, there for those who know when and how, and who also know that I do little to compromise the secrets of these fish by mentioning them here.

The season of harvest trout holds a solitude and intimacy instilled partly by the rivers themselves. Few of the streams that head in the coastal mountains are large or long. The close convolution of ridges and valleys splits the mountains into dozens of separate watersheds, each giving rise to its own river that finds its own passage to the sea. As rivers go, this is strikingly rare; most of them are but parts of something. Hike up to the remote third meadow of Slough Creek in Yellowstone, and no matter how it might seem, you're still fishing the Missouri. Pack into the high headwater streams of the Selway River, deep in the Idaho interior, and you still wade the Columbia. But the rivers of the coastal mountains are self-contained and individual, part of no larger drainage, each a distinct inhabitant of its own place. Perhaps not coincidentally, these identities are preserved in names. When white settlers came to Oregon in the last century, they made it theirs first by eradicating the Indians, then by exterminating any vestiges of Indian claims that persisted in the names of things. Only the coastal rivers (and then only some of them) resisted the authority of a new language. The Kilchis, Nehalem, Coquille, Neskowin, Tillamook, Siuslaw, Coos, Nestucca, Olalla, Necanicum, and others somehow defied the change and still flow under ancient words. I gravely doubt that the names were preserved out of any lingering respect or small feeling for the picturesque. Perhaps some inviolateness or singularity was vaguely sensed in these places, and it seemed best or safest to leave them alone.

The coastal rivers are each a part of nothing else, particularly located in a landscape, and this quality is shared by the trout. Unlike the salmon and steelhead that range over open ocean to distant coastlines, bluebacks seldom venture far from the estuary, at most a few miles, and though a true sea-run fish, they are unwilling to stray far from the land

and their home water. Harvest trout are the genius of the coastal rivers, the spirit of the place.

Massive transfusions of pre-dawn coffee are one part ritual, three parts necessity.

I've always taken great pleasure in arriving at the water by sun-up and beginning the day itself on the river, a carryover from my first days of trout fishing when I was hungry to be streamside every fishable minute. These days, rising before dawn is mostly habit, striking none of the second-order harmonics of self-righteous virtue for the simple reason that, now, it is easier to do than not. Then too, getting up early to fish ninety or a hundred days a year, although not much by the standards of a guide or outfitter, is enough to keep me in practice. Yet no matter how often I go fishing, I still sleep restlessly the night before a trip, waking often to check the clock and dreaming fitfully between times, my mind reeling with disjointed projections like cinema trailers or Sunday-night highlight films. It is a bit vain, I suppose, to admit that I've always been secretly a little proud of this, that the frequency of fishing has diluted neither the freshness nor anticipation of each occasion. A good night's sleep comes only after the trip—sometimes only after the season. When the harvest trout are in, I may pack up early and make the long, dark drive to the river three or four times a week. A month or so of this can leave you feeling pretty strung out and looking like it—an unshaven face with dark circles beneath red eyes, wired on the happy lunacy of sleep deprivation and fishing.

So rising early is hardly a penance, though what I rise into could be called "consciousness" only through an act of charity. Hence the infusion of early-morning coffee, one of the few legal substances capable of inducing that paradoxical condition of being almost asleep and wide awake at the same time.

Blueback season offers an additional incentive for getting on the road well before dawn. Perhaps the only constant about these unpredictable fish is that, under a bright sun, virtually nothing can induce them to strike. You can pray for an overcast sky—or a light drizzle since you're on your knees already—but this early in the fall, don't expect much of an answer. The best hope is to get on the river by dawn, when a thick fog hangs right down to the water and provides a passable substitute for clouds until it burns off in late morning.

In the calendar of the Wishram Indians, it is the month called "Travel-in-canoes-Moon," and in the dampness of 4:30 A.M., I hitch driftboat to truck and head toward the coast. Somewhere above the mist, the moon tugs a high tide from the ocean, and with it a harvest of trout. Along the highway, a few mud-flecked pickups and log-haulers nose into the halo of light around a diner; beyond them, the world shrinks to a tight yellow cocoon spun out of the vapor by my headlights. The drive is a slow one, made slower still by a large and witless population of coastal blacktail deer that react instinctively to the danger of oncoming cars by fleeing directly into their path. That the species has survived the industrial age is nothing short of miraculous.

I don't make the river until shortly before 6:00 A.M. and can see just well enough to shove the boat in. By the clock, it's after dawn, but beneath the fog, daybreak comes only as a sourceless slackening of the dark. The boat drifts in a globe of quarter-mile visibility whose edges diffuse into penumbral grayness. At high water, this blind-drifting would be dangerous; in the low flows of autumn, there is only the sense of existing at the center of some hazy corona, a damp membrane that has the weird revelatory power of sensory deprivation. The world contracts to a shell of small sounds that surround you—wavelets slapping the hull of the boat, deer moving in the woods, the wingbeats of an owl, a salmon rolling in the pool downriver, and above all the calls of geese overhead.

Certain specific sounds reach deep inside and back, atavisms grasped best by webbed and tailed embryos and primitive brainstems. I think of the tremolo of a loon, a timber wolf's howl, the scaly buzz of a rattlesnake, a thundering surf, the calls of Canada geese. As the recognition of autumn comes suddenly, in a moment, so one day you first hear the geese. Or rather, you first become aware of yourself hearing them. They may have been drifting above the mist, invisible as an assumption, for days or weeks, already pulling at something beneath consciousness with the distant, reedy sound of drones and chanters, piping a call as lonely as a border widow.

Bound for the south, these birds seem to me a strange point of fixity and resoluteness. Perhaps geese are the real geophysical constant, for in a sense they don't move at all. They take to altitudes to stay in one place, not migrating, but hovering, while the equinoctial tilting of the earth rocks the poles back and forth beneath them. The geese remain, an index of what used to be where, and of what will return again. Their seasonal appearance denotes your passing, not their own. In the estuaries, geese mingle with bluebacks and salmon and call to a world that just won't hold still.

The few other blueback fishermen out today will work the tidal stretches, pulling Ford Fenders or gang spinners behind too-heavy tackle and smoky outboards, unable to conceal the lethal boredom of trolling. Though I've cast flies in the estuary, there's too much undifferentiated water to search and too little time in the few hours of slack tide. Up the river, there's less company, less noise, more opportunity.

When it grows light enough, I begin casting. I know of no other fishing quite like this. Sea-run cutthroats often defy the conventional standards of river trout, shunning the moving water and congregating instead in deep, still pools, in the calm of bedrock bowls, along currentless dropoffs. Exhibiting a wild creature's affinity for edges, they are most at home on a deep bank shaded in overhanging brush or shielded by rocky ledges. Sometimes, particularly in low light, they betray their lies by rolling in abrupt and violent boils on the surface. These disturbances certainly aren't rises, nor, as far as I've determined, associated in any way with the capture of food. Perhaps the rolling is meant to stimulate something, the production of eggs or milt, or maybe to alleviate something, like scratching an itch. No one seems to know, but on a pool in early morning a dozen or more trout may churn the surface, each at its separate holding place along the bank.

So the bank is where you fish them, with a technique as particular to the bluebacks as these trout are indigenous to the region. The flies used surpass even the forty-second-street tackiness of most steelhead patterns, rivalling perhaps only the classic Atlantic salmon dressings in their ghastly flamboyancy. Fashioned from loud, unthinkable combinations of garishly dyed materials, they are dressed like a color-blind golfer, or one of the sleazy characters in a John Waters movie. In my earlier days as a spring-creek fisherman, I knew only the tiny, delicate insects of those waters, and my fly tying centered on replicating the subtle shades of color and sublime mottling of living creatures. Tying even a Royal Coachman seemed to me then an act of aesthetic vandalism, a grotesque violence perpetrated on a fly box. I have since adjusted my standards, though I still nurse no affection for fluorescent chenille, Day-Glo saddle hackle, and neon synthetics, and I keep this stuff (of which I possess an unholy amount) hidden out of sight in a cardboard box beneath my tying bench. Still, I need to have flies, and so once a year, seizing some moment of temporary perversity, I drag out the box and tie up a season's worth of these functional embarrassments.

For whatever reason, sea-run cutthroats show a decided preference for a certain shade of searing pink, next to which a flamingo is but a streak of gray mud. The color is found nowhere in nature, rarely even in the fishing world, and to my knowledge has been faithfully duplicated only by the manufacturers of certain polyester fabrics and, of course, by the great Pautzke himself. Hot yellows and purples rank a close second, and I must concede that flies dressed in combinations of these three hues outfish all others. Some fishermen argue that pink in particular triggers some residual memory in the fish, reminding it of the shrimp upon which it fed in saltwater. Little as I credit fish with anything like intelligence, even I can't buy this.

The only requirement aside from color is eight or ten wraps of soft, pliable hackle that produce, when wet, the impression of undulant respiration or beating cilia. The flies are fished wet, on a floating line, though not in the conventional down-and-across swing. Out in the boat, well toward the middle of the pool, you cast back at the bank and lay the fly as near as possible to dry land. This is not as simple as it sounds, often requiring a controlled, tight-looped cast that can carry the fly eight or ten feet back beneath overhanging branches. Inches make a critical difference. A reluctant or conservative caster who fails to reach the bank, fearful of hanging flies in the brush, catches nothing.

The retrieve is the other key. The fly sinks only an inch or two, remaining clearly visible just beneath the surface, and is worked to the boat in a series of short strips or twitches, with short pauses between. It must act like something lost and indecisive, hesitantly trying to find its way, yet desperately attempting to conceal its own conspicuousness. It must appear torn between the imperatives of an unobtrusive immobility and balls-out flight.

This requires a practiced imagination. It is a commonplace of angling that to catch fish, you must think like a predator, a vision of fishing that is really more like hunting, and sometimes true. Salmon and steelhead must be approached in just this way. But to fish trout, you must think like the prey and work a fly in the knowledge of how it feels to try to escape, to shrink yourself to insignificance in the face of impending threat when everything about you advertises your presence. Being the predator is exciting, but being the prey is a lot more like life and infinitely more interesting, since in the end, the prey sets the terms and so calls the shots.

In angling, the closest living relative of this technique is probably bass bugging, though the differences are still substantial. You never forget that you're on a river (forever more interesting to me than lakes) and that you're fishing trout, which are inherently less aggressive than bass. But most of all is the superb visualness of the entire affair from the moment the fly touches the water, and in this regard casting to bluebacks offers precisely the charm and fascination of dry-fly fishing. But standing in the boat, high over the water, your vantage point is even better. Suddenly and out of nowhere, a trout appears in the water behind the fly, fins splayed and aggressively rigid, and from above it looks like a small, blue shark. Whether the fish only follows the fly, or nips it, or slashes at it, the whole episode is played out right before your eyes. Though in its techniques, flies, and types of water, blueback fishing is about as distant as you can get from spring-creek angling, the vibes of the experience are remarkably similar.

Harvest trout have one other distinct peculiarity. No other fish I know of has such a consistent propensity for striking short; their ability to seize a fly momentarily, charge a short distance, and simply let it go, borders on the supernatural. As anatomies go, trout lips never seemed to me a particularly nimble arrangement, though I'm in the process of revising this opinion. A good day on sea-run cutts is measured in follows and strikes, not hooked fish.

That they take flies at all is something of an enigma. Their predominant freshwater food appears to be crayfish, and the timing of the run coincides with a substantial number of these crustaceans in the river. In fall, the crayfish turn bright orange; drifting over the clear water, you can easily pick them out on the bottom, as conspicuous as tiny boiled lobsters or waterlogged maple leaves. Upriver, later in the season when the salmon arrive, some bluebacks will hold downstream of spawning salmon and snatch up eggs that tumble out of the redd. But in these still pools, crayfish seem the item of choice, and more often than not, you can feel the faint crunch of a half-digested exoskeleton in a fat-bellied blueback landed by hand. I hasten to add that flies dressed to imitate crayfish almost invariably fail.

On a stretch of river I used to float often, I sometimes ran into a fellow about ten years older than myself, a local who set a string of crayfish traps, seventy in all, doled out along the pools and deep spots in groups of fours and fives. He ran the string, he said, every other morning, putting the big ones in a live box and the small ones in a bucket, and rebaiting the traps with canned dog food. He couldn't stand to eat crayfish, he said, and couldn't afford to even if he liked them because they brought a nice price from a fish house in Portland. When he finished tending the traps, he rowed his wooden skiff to a big bend-pool, hooked a small crayfish in the tail, and fished for harvest trout (he never once called them bluebacks), often falling asleep in the boat and not waking up until early afternoon. Over the course of our chance meetings, he revealed that later in the season he fished for salmon a bit, but mostly went out to the woods, to special places he knew, and picked wild mushrooms. He sold them to a buyer in Kernville who, he said with some pride, shipped them by jet twice a week to restaurants back East. Some days he set out crab pots in the bay on ebb tide, or walked the muddy flats at low slack and dug softshells and butter clams, or pumped sand shrimp to sell for bait.

When winter came, he hiked the back ridges looking for shed elk antlers, which he sold to a man who ground them up and sent them across the Pacific, where they were sold again to enhance a multitude of erections. If he needed cash, he said, he jobbed out in the woods, working for gyppo outfits, or stripping yew bark, even once cutting cedar boughs for Christmas wreaths, though these jobs never lasted long, he confessed, which was fine with him. He seemed to know all there was to know about the rivers and mountains of the coast, and how to live on them and how to live off them, and in small ways he cobbled together a contented existence as a born scavenger, a crayfish of a man.

I haven't run into him for a few years, and what stands out to me now is not how eccentric he was, but how typical, how he embodied a kind of native eclecticism rooted in the place and people. Along the rivers up and down the coast, yarn-dyed rednecks and fourth-generation locals are neighbors to the toasted leftovers of hippiedom who retreated west from the valley and north from California. They in turn live alongside younger versions of themselves, Birkenstocked organic farmers with woodstoves and espresso machines, meticulously tending some stern dream.

Despite the newcomers, the land has the look of a place settled all at once, once and for all, resistant to wholesale change but refitting itself in small ways, in bits and pieces, so that houses and homesteads have become almost uniformly miscellaneous. On his first trip here to fish, my brother proposed that Oregon be renamed "the homemade state." One-room frame cabins built long ago, and now outgrown, have their seams let out, in time acquiring ad hoc alterations and additions, a room stuck on here or there, half a second story with an unfinished balcony, a rickety shed hauled in from somewhere else and left near the house to store wood. A neglected lean-to outside the kitchen is patched up as an awning for a new fiberglass hot tub. Propped on screwjacks and sheltered under a makeshift roof, an ancient house-trailer streaked with rust sprouts a wooden porch and carport. An unused machine shed is dismantled and the boards burned to clear the concrete pad for a satellite dish. And all of it is done with the kind of heedlessness that comes in a place where wood is cheap and available and the winters never very cold.

Outside, scattered around within striking distance of some theoretical purpose, are rusting rolls of barbed wire, stacks of weathered lumber, oil drums and angle iron, and an assortment of third-hand machinery. A wood-hauling trailer, fashioned from the bed of a venerable pickup, is tipped upside down and spray-painted red, a dry place for the dogs. A diesel engine wrestled from a rusting tractor powers a little water pump; next to it, a 1949 International school bus, converted to crude domesticity, lives its middle years as a makeshift RV with propane bottles and water tanks strapped to the bumper. When it finally stops running, it will be retired as a home for dirt bikes and rototillers wheeled up a ramp through the emergency door, or its windows painted black to conceal the lights of a little subsistence marijuana farming. A few goats tethered at the edge of the yard nibble back the Himalaya vine that would otherwise, in a season or two, swallow up the whole place.

It is tempting to dismiss them as all squalid and seedy, which they more or less are, but I see in these places as well a kind of native, extemporaneous architecture, born of the sense that things and structures, like people and rivers, live lives of change. This particular object is a milk van only because it started out that way; over time, it will become a boat shed, then a chicken coop, then a source of aluminum sheathing, and finally, a vine-covered windfall for bobcats and yellow jackets.

Within it all is the idea that stability is not the same as stasis, and at least in this respect, the self-contained, improvisational spaces that people make here are an expression of the landscape itself. They are, like the envelope of fog on a fall morning, or the chevrons of geese overhead, or the crayfish trapper, or the run of harvest trout, or the singularity of a coastal river, one of the small wholenesses that are to me the essence of this place.

The fishing here is invariably superb; always, it's the catching that's up for grabs. Today, after a strong high tide and a fog that lingers as a thin film into the afternoon, even the catching is pretty fair. In all the proven places—the Christmas Tree Hole, the Ledges, Feedbag, Hourglass Pool—I find fish, hooking fewer than I turn, landing fewer than I hook. Some are the river's resident cutthroat; most are sea-runs, easily distinguished by their silvery sides, the paleness of red on the gill slash, their larger size and disproportionate strength. Even in the river, they have an ocean's power behind them.

A sixteen-inch fish is a good one, and I've caught them larger, but not often. Most average about fourteen inches, and although most days you catch average fish, there are really no average days. In each one, small essences are implanted. A bright summer steelhead rises from the opaque depths of the pool in smooth, vertical levitation, like a hot air balloon, and touches the fly with its nose, but will not take. Five elk stand chest-deep in the river, ambling ashore as I drift down, and moments later a camouflaged bowhunter with a painted face sneaks along the bank, raising a finger to his lips to silence my approach. On a bright afternoon, hundreds of butterflies, migrating to somewhere, swarm above the river; some rest to drink in a patch of damp sand at the water's edge, and a small trout charges them like an orca hunting seals in the surf. A barechested young man fishes from the bank, an Indian from Siletz with a thick, black ponytail, a gymnast's build, and a fierce tattoo on each brown bicep. As I float past, he reaches into the grass and with one finger hoists an enormous hen chinook as if it were a herring. Under a warm rain, two old women face one another at opposite ends of a dented canoe, with wet, denimed legs outstretched in the bottom; they giggle and swear happily as the canoe spins one lazy circle after another in the slow current.

Events and images like these, rooted in some intrinsic completeness of the moment, are the seed-bearing fruit of the season. And if there is any "art" in fishing, it has to do with this, rather than the tying of flies or the graceful geometries of casting. In the end, to fish well is to cultivate an arrangement of time and place, of circumstance and perspective. We arrange ourselves into the arrangement, and if the collusion is careful and lucky, we reap a kind of enclosed moment of some sharply felt beauty and significance. The particularities of river and landscape, of the trout and the season, of the fisherman and the fishing, all merge, crystallizing the instant into a whole that exceeds the sum of its parts, the way a musical chord, with high tones and low ones struck at once, pushes back the borders of simultaneity and creates within the space of harmony. To drift down a coastal river in autumn is just such a chord, played for an audience of one.

Fishing is commonly, and mistakenly I believe, regarded as a form of escapism. But it seems to me more closely allied with a deeper historical impulse, a submerged conviction in the national consciousness from the very beginning that some new and improved brand of the self can be reinvented in the fresher air of uncorrupted places, where the best things will flourish and the worst die of inanition. The path of American history is strewn with the remains of noble, foolish visions and doomed utopian experiments, from Puritanism, to Brook Farm and Oneida, to Marin County communes—continual rediscoveries that there is no perfect world, no matter how small you shrink it. There are, I think, only moments of local perfection, fashioned from design and chance. Robert Frost once asked, "What to make of a diminished thing?" A harvest of these brief entireties appears to me a plausible response, perhaps the only one. A life lived recollecting or creating or anticipating such moments, enjoying and appreciating their value, may not possess the seamless continuity that we expect of something like "truth," but it does have the feel of some truthlike substance. And I'll settle for that.

In the afternoon, a sea-breeze rises. Along the coast, you can see the shape of moving air in wind-carved trees and dunes. It looks remarkably like the shape of moving water. The wind finally drops when the sun does, and the fishing picks up again. I rarely keep trout any more, but today I keep one sea-run cutthroat. It too is a kind of harvest of the year, though not in the sense that fishery technicians and forest managers speak of "harvesting the resource," with its overtones of benign proprietorship. Trout are not a crop to be picked like oranges. I catch a fish and bury the point of a knife deep into the base of its skull. Lying in a cooler at my feet, it is not "harvested"—it is emphatically dead, lying gel-eyed on a block of ice, an equivocal prolongation of the day and season put in cold storage.

At dusk, the air thickens again into a chilly fog. Flights of geese descend from everywhere, converging on the estuary to roost, their voices sharp and sad as the tang of fallen apples. They will go on like this, flying and calling, far past sunset, gradually becoming invisible in the mist and twilight, until at last there is only a chevron sound that folds down around you like a pair of enormous gray wings.